Baking

All Year Round

ROSANNA PANSINO

sphere

SPHERE

Copyright © 2018 by Milk Carton Entertainment

First published in the United States in 2018 by Atria Books, an imprint of Simon & Schuster, Inc.
First published in Great Britain in 2018 by Sphere

Writing by Rosanna Pansino

Cover and principal photography by Michael Schmidt

3 5 7 9 10 8 6 4

The moral right of the author has been asserted.

A CIP catalogue record for this book is available from the British Library.

ISBN 978-0-7515-7400-5

Printed in Italy

Papers used by Sphere are from well-managed forests and other responsible sources

MIX
Paper from
responsible sources
FSC® C104740
www.fsc.org

Sphere
An imprint of
Little, Brown Book Group
Carmelite House
50 Victoria Embankment
London EC4Y 0DZ

An Hachette UK Company
www.hachette.co.uk

www.littlebrown.co.uk

This book is dedicated to my mom and dad, for
making every holiday a special occasion. Thank you
for working so hard to create lifelong memories.

CONTENTS

INTRODUCTION

BAKING IS MY LOVE LANGUAGE. I adore creating themed desserts for the holidays and any special occasion. Many of my favorite childhood memories took place in the kitchen with family and friends. My grandma taught me to cook and bake starting at a very young age. I would spend time with her making things like fresh pasta, desserts, and dinners.

My parents always wanted the holidays to be memorable for my sister and me, so they worked extra hard to make sure that happened every year. Whether it was inviting the whole family for Christmas or having all of our friends over for a Halloween party, they found a way to make each season special and bring people together with food. Two of my favorite family dessert recipes are included in this book. In the summertime, my mom would make this fresh Blackberry Cobbler (page 92) and for Christmas, the world's best Gingerbread Man Cookies (page 164).

My dad is especially fond of Christmas. For over twenty years, he dressed up like Santa Claus and volunteered his time at children's hospitals and events to help spread holiday cheer. Mom and Dad also make the most adorable Mr. and Mrs. Claus, which they still dress up as.

Being inspired by them, my sister and I used to dress up like Santa and a reindeer and then run around the house pretending to deliver presents. Our love of celebrating holidays has always been a part of my life, which is why I wanted to make a book full of recipes that are important to me.

In each chapter of this book, you will find recipes for many of the holidays and special occasions that my family celebrates, such as Christmas, New Year's, Valentine's Day, birthdays, Mother's Day, Father's Day, and more. I hope it can be your guide for years to come with fun, creative, and delicious ideas to make and share. Whether you're headed to a last-minute party or have plenty of time to prepare, this book has everything you'll need to make a lasting impression. I've also sprinkled in several recipes that are either gluten-free, dairy-free, or vegan, so there's something for everyone to enjoy and celebrate all year round!

My Mom   My Aunt Pat   My Grandma Nana

Making Handmade Ravioli

My Dad, Papa Pizza

My Mom, Mama Mia

My sister Molly as a Reindeer

Dressing Up as Santa

HOW TO USE THIS BOOK

RECIPE ICONS

This book includes many recipes that are gluten-free, dairy-free, or vegan. I've marked them with the below icons. When you see an icon on a recipe it applies to the entire recipe, which includes the frostings and candies used.

GLUTEN-FREE

DAIRY-FREE

VEGAN

ICINGS, FROSTINGS, & TOPPINGS

All of the made-from-scratch icings, frostings, and toppings used in this book are included on pages 16–21.

STEP-BY-STEP PHOTOS

I have added step-by-step photos to recipes that are better understood with additional pictures. These photos are each labeled with letters to match their corresponding steps in the recipe and can be used as a visual guide.

TEMPLATES

Some of the recipes in this book use cookie cutters and fun shapes. Most templates to re-create these shapes have been included on pages 248–251.

To make a stencil, trace the desired shape onto a piece of paper and then cut it out with scissors. Once you have the shape cut out, simply place it on your rolled out dough or fondant and use a small knife to cut around the edges.

For recipes that require a drawn template, trace copies of your desired shape onto a sheet of paper and then place wax paper over the top to cover it. Pipe royal icing, melted chocolate, or Candy Melts on top of the wax paper and let set until hardened. Once dry, gently remove them by hand or by carefully sliding a sharp knife underneath.

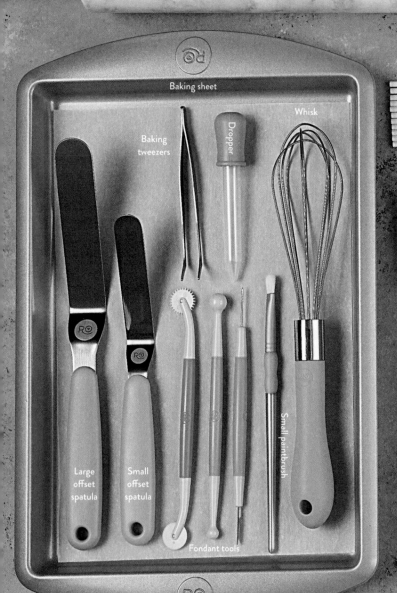

Rolling pin

Lollipop sticks

Baking sheet

Whisk

Baking tweezers

Dropper

Wooden spoon

Spatula

Pastry brush

Small paintbrush

Serrated knife

Large offset spatula

Small offset spatula

Fondant tools

Baking scissors

Toothpicks

Stand mixer

Decorating tips

Metal horn

Whisk attachment

809   829

1A   824

2A   1M   2D   366

12   4B   30   352

10   32   233

Paddle attachment

Hook attachment

5   21

4   18

Wire rack

Candy thermometer

3   16

2   14

1

°F   °C

380   200
deep
180
340
160
hard crack
300
140
hard ball
soft crack
260
120
soft ball
thread
220
100

Sieve

Decorating bags

180   80

140   60

CANDY

Reese's Pieces

Dark chocolate coating wafers

White chocolate coating wafers

Peanut Butter Cups Miniatures

M&M's Minis

Chocolate chips

White chocolate chips

Peanut Butter Cups Minis

Mini chocolate chips

Mini marshmallows

Milk Duds

Cadbury Mini Eggs

Chocolate crisp pearls

Red chip crunch sprinkles

Chocolate square

Tootsie Rolls

Caramels

Pecan halves

Walnuts

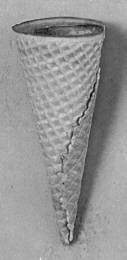

OREOs

Pretzel sticks

Peanuts

Ice cream cone

Crispy rice cereal

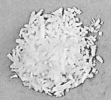

Shredded coconut

Star sprinkles

Brach's Jelly Beans

Gummy bears

Edible pink pearls

Edible white pearls

Hot Tamales

Candy corn

Edible blue pearls

Nonpareils

Red Hots

Small & large candy eyeballs

Good & Plenty

Edible silver pearls

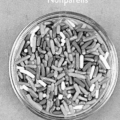

Sprinkles

Crushed peppermint

SweeTARTS

Edible gold pearls

Confetti sprinkles

Edible gold stars

Banana Laffy Taffy

Black FoodWriter pen

Edible light pink pearls

Blue sanding sugar

Pink sanding sugar

Fine & coarse gold sanding sugar

White sanding sugar

TERMINOLOGY

MELTING

There are several methods to melt chocolate, candy, or butter.

MICROWAVE: Heat for short amounts of time in a microwave-safe bowl, stirring between each interval. Repeat until fully melted. Microwaves are the fastest way to melt ingredients.

DOUBLE BOILER: Place a heat-safe bowl on top of a pan of simmering water, leaving enough space so that the bottom of the bowl isn't touching the water. Continue to simmer and stir until fully melted. Double boilers have a much lower chance of burning chocolate.

MELTING POT: Using a melting pot, keep at a constant temperature to maintain desired consistency. Melting pots are great for dipping treats and cake pops.

PEAKS

When beating egg whites or heavy cream, peaks are formed when the beater is lifted out of the mixture. These are used to determine its current consistency. The longer you beat, the stiffer the peaks become.

SOFT PEAK: The peak is soft and the tip will fold back on itself immediately.

FIRM (MEDIUM) PEAK: The peak will hold, but the tip will slightly fold back on itself.

STIFF PEAK: The peak will hold and the tip points straight up.

OVERBEATEN: The peak will eventually collapse back on itself. The mixture will also look grainy and dull.

FOLD: Gently combining a delicate mixture with a thicker one. This allows them to blend together while maintaining the air in the mixture and also helps prevent overmixing. Folding is often done with a wooden spoon or rubber spatula.

BEAT: Mixing rapidly to combine ingredients to become a smooth texture. Beating can be done with a wooden spoon, whisk, electric hand mixer, or stand mixer.

WHISK: Blending soft or liquid ingredients together quickly and incorporating air with vigorous mixing. Can be done more gently when used for just dry ingredients. Whisking is usually done with a wire whisk.

SIFT: Passing dry ingredients through a mesh sieve or sifter to incorporate air and filter out chunks and impurities.

STIR: Mixing ingredients together using a figure-eight or circular motion until well combined or a uniform consistency.

BLOOM GELATIN: Soaking powdered gelatin in cool water for 3 to 5 minutes to soften before using. This helps ensure a smoother consistency for the recipe.

POACH: Gently cooking food submerged in a liquid at low temperature.

FROTHY EGGS: Beating eggs until no liquid is left at the bottom of the bowl. Stop once they look bubbly and opaque, otherwise soft peaks will begin to form.

CRUMB COAT: Applying a thin first layer of frosting on a cake to catch loose crumbs and prevent them from showing once fully iced. Refrigerate before applying the final frosting layer. This helps create a smooth and even finish.

Royal Icing

MAKES 2½ CUPS

3 large egg whites
4 cups powdered sugar
¼ teaspoon cream of tartar
1 teaspoon honey
¼ teaspoon salt
¼ teaspoon vanilla extract

1. In a large bowl, with an electric mixer, beat the egg whites, powdered sugar, and cream of tartar until thick and smooth, 5 to 6 minutes.
2. Beat in the honey, salt, and vanilla until smooth, about 1 minute.

Vegan Royal Icing

MAKES 2 CUPS

4 cups powdered sugar, sifted
6 tablespoons liquid from canned chickpeas
1 teaspoon vanilla extract
½ teaspoon almond extract
Pinch of salt

1. In a large bowl, with an electric mixer, beat the powdered sugar and chickpea liquid until smooth and thick, 4 to 5 minutes.
2. Beat in the vanilla, almond extract, and salt until well combined, 1 to 2 minutes.

> ○ RO **TIP** ○

TO THIN THE ICING
Add ½ teaspoon water at a time.

TO THICKEN THE ICING
Add 1 tablespoon
powdered sugar at a time.

ICINGS

Swiss Buttercream Frosting

MAKES 5 CUPS

5 large egg whites
1 cup granulated sugar
1 cup powdered sugar
¼ teaspoon cream of tartar
1 teaspoon vanilla extract
4 sticks (16 ounces) unsalted butter, at room
  temperature

Equipment
Heatproof bowl
Stand mixer fitted with the whisk attachment

1. Fill a medium saucepan with 1 inch of water and bring to a simmer.
2. In a medium heatproof bowl, whisk together the egg whites, granulated sugar, powdered sugar, cream of tartar, and vanilla until combined.
3. Place the bowl over the simmering water, making sure the bottom of the bowl doesn't touch the water. Whisk until the mixture is warm and the sugar has dissolved.
4. Pour the mixture into a stand mixer fitted with the whisk attachment and beat on high speed until the mixture cools to room temperature, 15 to 20 minutes.
5. On low speed, slowly add the butter 1 tablespoon at a time until fully combined. Scrape down the sides and bottom of the bowl as needed.

Vegan Buttercream Frosting

MAKES 2 CUPS

½ cup butter-flavored shortening
8 tablespoons vegan butter
2½ cups powdered sugar, sifted
Pinch of salt
½ teaspoon vanilla extract
1 teaspoon almond extract
1 tablespoon unsweetened almond milk

1. In a large bowl, with an electric mixer, beat the shortening and vegan butter until smooth, 2 to 3 minutes.
2. Add the powdered sugar 1 cup at a time, beating well after each addition. Scrape down the sides and bottom of the bowl as needed.
3. Beat in the salt, vanilla, almond extract, and almond milk until creamy, 3 to 5 minutes.

Champagne Frosting

MAKES 4 CUPS

4 large egg whites
1 cup sugar
1 cup flat champagne (no carbonation)
4 sticks (16 ounces) unsalted butter, cubed,
   at room temperature
¼ teaspoon salt

Equipment
Stand mixer fitted with the whisk attachment
Candy thermometer

1. In a stand mixer fitted with the whisk
   attachment, whip the egg whites on medium
   speed until frothy, 1 to 2 minutes.
2. In a small saucepan fitted with a candy
   thermometer, whisk the sugar and ½ cup of the
   champagne. Place over medium-low heat until
   the mixture reaches 200°F.
3. With the mixer on low speed, slowly pour the
   sugar mixture into the egg whites. Whip on
   high speed until the mixture and bowl have
   cooled to room temperature, 15 to 20 minutes.
4. On low speed, slowly add the butter
   1 tablespoon at a time until fully combined.
   Scrape down the sides and bottom of the
   bowl as needed.
5. Add the remaining ½ cup champagne and the
   salt and whip on medium speed until light and
   fluffy, 5 to 6 minutes.

Cream Cheese Frosting

MAKES 4 CUPS

1 package (8 ounces) cream cheese, at room
   temperature
2 sticks (8 ounces) unsalted butter, at room
   temperature
5 cups powdered sugar, sifted
¼ teaspoon salt
1 teaspoon vanilla extract
⅛ teaspoon almond extract

1. In a large bowl, with an electric mixer, beat the
   cream cheese until smooth, about 1 minute.
2. Beat in the butter until well combined, 2 to 3
   minutes.
3. Add the powdered sugar 1 cup at a time, mixing
   well after each addition. Scrape down the sides
   and bottom of the bowl as needed.
4. Beat in the salt, vanilla, and almond extract
   until well combined, about 2 minutes.

Dark Chocolate Frosting

MAKES 3 CUPS

2 sticks (8 ounces) unsalted butter, at room
   temperature
2 tablespoons honey
2 teaspoons vanilla extract
1 teaspoon salt
1½ cups unsweetened dark cocoa powder (Hershey's
   Special Dark), sifted
3 cups powdered sugar, sifted
½ cup whole milk

1. In a large bowl, with an electric mixer, beat the
    butter, honey, vanilla, salt, and cocoa powder
    until well combined, 3 to 4 minutes.
2. Add the powdered sugar 1 cup at a time,
    beating well after each addition. Scrape down
    the sides and bottom of the bowl as needed.
3. Beat in the milk until the frosting is smooth and
    fluffy, 3 to 4 minutes.

Honey Buttercream Frosting

MAKES 4 CUPS

1 cup honey
4 large egg whites
3 sticks (12 ounces) unsalted butter, cut into cubes
   and chilled
2 teaspoons vanilla extract
¼ teaspoon salt

Equipment
Candy thermometer
Stand mixer fitted with the whisk attachment

1. In a small saucepan fitted with a candy
    thermometer, heat the honey to 240°F over
    medium heat.
2. In a stand mixer fitted with the whisk
    attachment, whip the egg whites on medium
    speed until soft peaks form, 3 to 5 minutes.
3. On low speed, slowly pour the honey into the
    egg whites. Beat on high speed until the mixture
    cools to room temperature, 15 to 20 minutes.
4. On low speed, slowly add the butter
    1 tablespoon at a time until fully combined.
    Scrape down the sides and bottom of the
    bowl as needed.
5. Beat in the vanilla and salt on medium speed
    until light and fluffy, about 3 minutes.

Vegan Caramel Sauce

MAKES 1 CUP

1 can (11.25 ounces) sweetened condensed coconut milk
4 tablespoons vegetable shortening
¼ cup water

1. In a small saucepan, combine the condensed coconut milk, shortening, and water and bring to a boil over medium-high heat.
2. Reduce the heat to medium-low and simmer, stirring every couple of minutes, until the mixture begins to thicken and turn an amber color, 20 to 22 minutes.
3. Remove from the heat and let cool before using.

Whipped Cream

MAKES 2½ CUPS

1½ cups heavy cream
2 tablespoons sugar
½ teaspoon vanilla extract
Pinch of salt

In a large bowl, with an electric mixer, beat the heavy cream, sugar, vanilla, and salt until stiff peaks form, about 3 minutes.

· RO **TIP** ·

If your whipped cream is
TOO THIN, whip it longer
to thicken.

White Chocolate Glaze

MAKES 1 CUP

1 cup white chocolate chips
⅓ cup heavy cream
1 teaspoon light corn syrup
2 teaspoons white food coloring

1. Melt together the white chocolate chips, heavy cream, and corn syrup, stirring occasionally until smooth.
2. Stir in the white food coloring until well combined.
3. Use the glaze while still warm, but not hot.

White Chocolate Pouring Fondant

MAKES 5 CUPS

1½ cups white chocolate chips
4½ cups powdered sugar, sifted
¼ cup light corn syrup
6 tablespoons hot water
1 teaspoon vanilla extract
¼ teaspoon almond extract

1. Melt the chocolate chips.
2. In a large bowl, mix the powdered sugar, corn syrup, hot water, vanilla, and almond extract until smooth.
3. Fold in the melted chocolate until well combined.
4. Use the fondant while still warm, but not hot.

> RO **TIP**

If the pouring fondant
is TOO THICK TO POUR,
thin it by stirring in 1 teaspoon
water at a time.

♥

CHAPTER ONE

VALENTINE'S DAY

XOXO CHURROS

Whether you are celebrating Valentine's Day with your family, friends, or that special someone, these churros are a great gift to make and share with those you love. Hugs and kisses!

THE THINGS YOU'LL NEED

Churros
About 8 cups vegetable oil, for deep-frying
1 cup water
2 tablespoons granulated sugar
¼ teaspoon salt
2 tablespoons coconut oil
1 cup all-purpose flour
½ teaspoon baking powder
1 large egg

Decoration
Fine sanding sugars: red and white

Equipment
Candy thermometer
#2D decorating tip

LET'S GET STARTED!

1. In a large pot fitted with a candy thermometer, heat 4 inches of vegetable oil to 375°F over medium heat.
2. In a medium saucepan, whisk together the water, granulated sugar, salt, and coconut oil and bring to a boil over high heat.
3. In a small bowl, whisk together the flour and baking powder.
4. Add the flour mixture to the saucepan and stir constantly over high heat until combined and the dough pulls away from the sides of the pan, 1 to 2 minutes.
5. Transfer the dough to a medium bowl. With an electric mixer, beat the dough until it cools slightly and no steam rises, about 1 minute.
6. Add the egg and beat until the dough is shiny and smooth, 2 to 3 minutes.

TIME TO DECORATE!

1. Line a baking sheet with wax paper.
2. Scoop the dough into a decorating bag fitted with a #2D tip. Pipe 3-inch X's and O's onto the wax paper.
3. Freeze the churros until firm, 10 to 15 minutes.
4. When the oil has reached 375°F, carefully place a few churros into the hot oil (don't crowd the pan) and fry on both sides until golden brown, 1 to 2 minutes per side.
5. Place the churros on paper towels to drain and cool slightly, 2 to 5 minutes.
6. While the churros are still slightly warm, toss them in the sanding sugars: red for the X's and white for the O's.

CONVERSATION HEART
PETITS FOURS

A petit four is a bite-size French pastry. These mini cakes are glazed with pouring fondant and decorated to look like the iconic Valentine's Day conversation heart candies. You can get creative and decorate them with any expression you'd like.

THE THINGS YOU'LL NEED

Candy Heart Chiffon Cake
1½ cups all-purpose flour
1 teaspoon baking powder
½ teaspoon baking soda
½ teaspoon salt
1½ cups sugar
½ cup water
½ cup vegetable oil
1½ teaspoons vanilla extract
Seeds of ½ vanilla bean
6 large eggs, separated
⅓ cup tart candies (SweeTARTS),
    finely crushed

Filling
1 batch Swiss Buttercream Frosting
    (page 17)
½ cup seedless raspberry jam

Decorations
2 batches White Chocolate
    Pouring Fondant (page 21)
Food coloring: white, pink, orange,
    yellow, green, blue, purple, and
    red
1 batch Royal Icing (page 16)

Equipment
Heart biscuit cutter: 2 x 2½ inches,
    1½ inches deep (template on
    page 248)
#1 decorating tip

LET'S GET STARTED!

1. Preheat the oven to 350°F. Grease four 9 x 13-inch rimmed baking sheets and line them with parchment paper.
2. Make the chiffon cake: In a large bowl, whisk together the flour, baking powder, baking soda, and salt.
3. In a medium bowl, whisk together 1 cup of the sugar, the water, oil, vanilla extract, vanilla seeds, and egg yolks. Pour the sugar mixture into the flour mixture and whisk until well combined.
4. In a large bowl, with an electric mixer, beat the egg whites until frothy, about 4 minutes. Continue beating, slowly adding the remaining ½ cup sugar until stiff peaks form.
5. Fold one-third of the egg whites into the batter and mix until well combined. Repeat two more times. Fold in the crushed candies.
6. Divide the batter evenly among the prepared baking sheets and spread it evenly. Bake for 16 to 18 minutes, until the cakes are firm to the touch, switching the pans from top to bottom and rotating them front to back halfway through.
7. Let cool in the pans for 15 minutes, then turn out onto wire racks to cool completely.
8. For the filling: Make the Swiss Buttercream Frosting.

• CONTINUES •

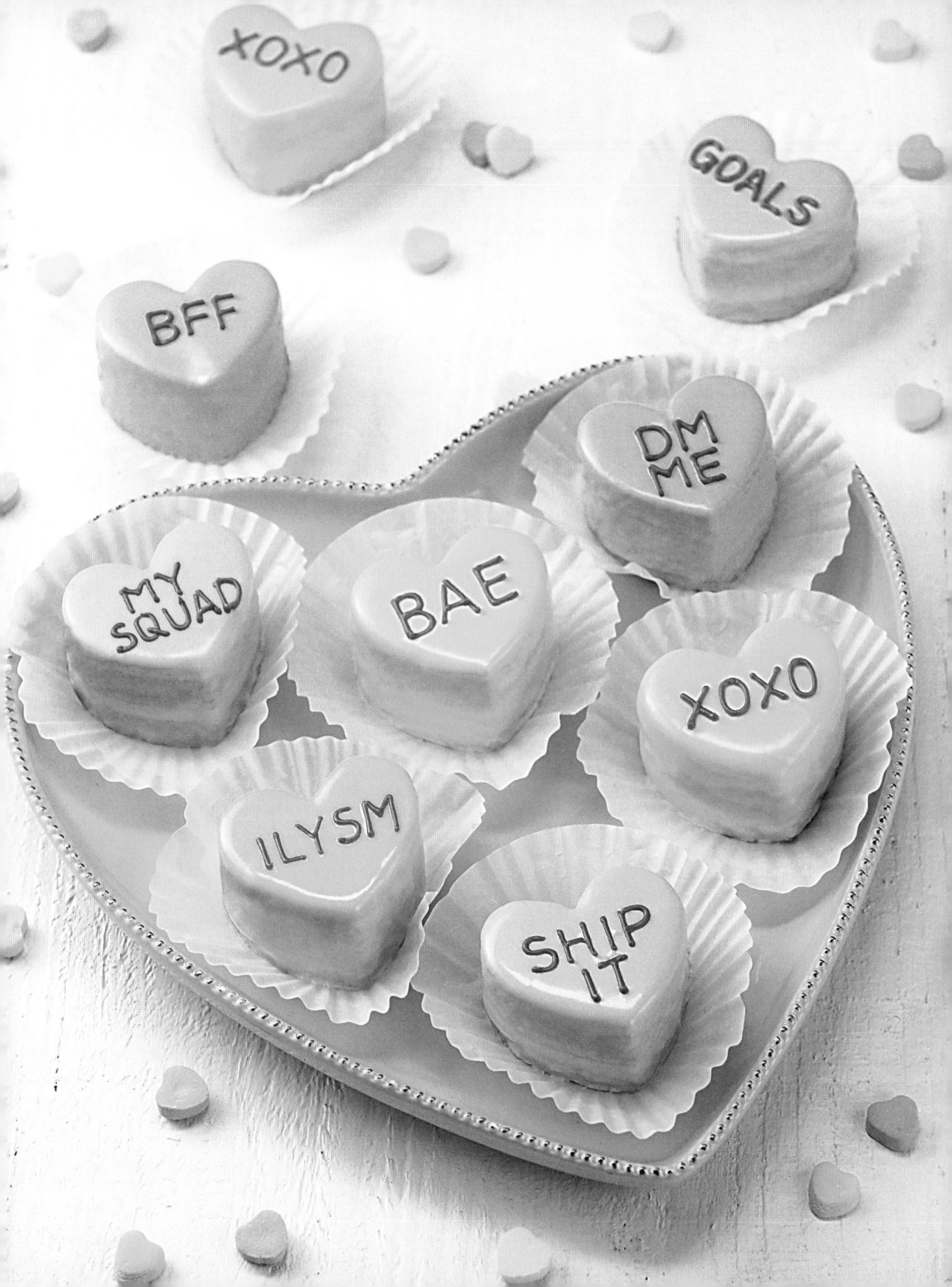
XOXO
GOALS
BFF
DM ME
MY SQUAD
BAE
XOXO
ILYSM
SHIP IT

LET'S GET STARTED! (CONTINUED)

9. Stack the cakes on parchment, alternating the filling between them in this order: jam, frosting, jam, and top with frosting **A**.
10. Refrigerate the cake for 30 minutes.
11. Cut out individual heart cakes using the heart biscuit cutter **B**.

TIME TO DECORATE!

1. Make the White Chocolate Pouring Fondant and mix in 1½ teaspoons white food coloring. Divide the fondant among 6 bowls. Tint each bowl with a different food coloring: pink, orange, yellow, green, blue, and purple.
2. Set one-sixth of the heart cakes on a wire rack over parchment paper. Using a heatproof measuring cup with a spout, pour one of the fondant colors over the cakes **C**.
3. Repeat with the remaining fondant colors and cakes.
4. Let the fondant dry, about 30 minutes.
5. Make the Royal Icing. Tint red and scoop into a decorating bag fitted with a #1 tip.
6. Pipe messages onto each heart petit four **D**.

RO TIP

Dip the cutter in hot water for a SMOOTHER cut.

RO TIP

COAT each cake twice. If necessary, strain the excess fondant for crumbs and use it again.

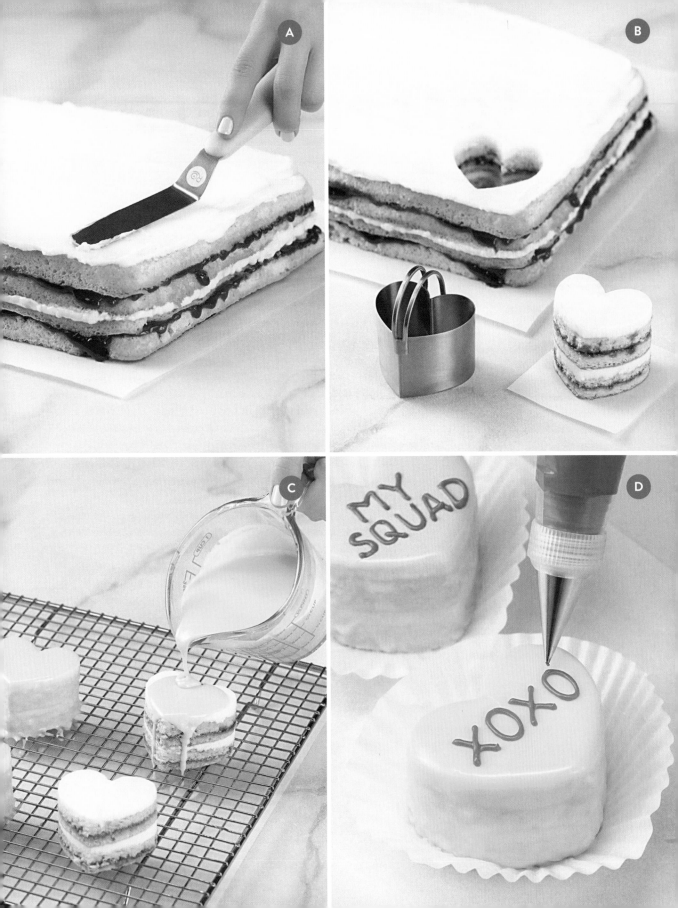

HEART
SOFT PRETZELS

If you want to make a savory treat for your sweetie, homemade soft pretzels are a great choice. Especially when they are baked with love and served fresh out of the oven.

THE THINGS YOU'LL NEED

Pretzel Dough
1 envelope (¼ ounce) active dry yeast
½ cup warm water
2 tablespoons honey
½ cup pale ale beer, at room temperature
2 teaspoons sugar
2 tablespoons unsalted butter, melted
2 cups bread flour
¾ cup all-purpose flour
1 teaspoon salt
1 tablespoon olive oil, for coating the bowl and dough

Poaching Liquid
10 cups water
½ cup baking soda

Topping
3 tablespoons unsalted butter, melted
¼ cup coarse salt

Equipment
Stand mixer fitted with the dough hook

LET'S GET STARTED!

1. Make the pretzel dough: In the bowl of a stand mixer fitted with the dough hook, whisk together the yeast, warm water, and honey. Set aside until foamy, about 10 minutes. Once foamy, stir in the beer, sugar, and melted butter.
2. In a medium bowl, whisk together the bread flour and all-purpose flour.
3. On low speed, stir ½ cup of the flour mixture into the yeast mixture until a thick paste forms.
4. On low speed, beat in the salt and remaining flour ½ cup at a time. Mix until the dough is soft and pulls away from the sides of the bowl, 3 to 5 minutes.
5. On a lightly floured surface, knead the dough for an additional minute. If the dough is too sticky, add more flour as needed. Form into a large ball.
6. Grease a large bowl with the olive oil and place the dough inside. Roll the dough in the oil to completely coat. Cover the bowl with a clean cloth and let rest at room temperature until doubled in size, 1 to 2 hours.
7. Line 3 baking sheets with parchment paper and lightly grease the paper.
8. Divide the dough into 15 portions and shape each portion into a ball. Keep the dough covered with a clean cloth to prevent a skin from forming.

• CONTINUES •

9. Shape each pretzel by rolling the dough ball into a 12-inch rope. Bring the two ends up to meet and form a circle. Twist and pinch the ends of the rope together and fold the joined ends down into the center of the circle to form a heart (A). Pinch the dough at the bottom to create the heart point (B). Gently place on the baking sheet. Repeat with the remaining dough.

10. Cover the shaped dough with a clean cloth and let rest for 10 to 15 minutes to proof.

11. Preheat the oven to 375°F.

12. While the dough is resting, prepare the poaching liquid: In a large pot, combine the water and baking soda and bring to about 160°F (not boiling) over medium heat.

13. Poach each pretzel for 30 seconds on each side, flipping with a slotted spoon or sieve (C). Once poached, place on the prepared baking sheets. This step creates the iconic pretzel taste and texture.

14. Top the pretzels: Brush with the melted butter (D) and sprinkle with coarse salt.

15. Bake until golden brown, 12 to 15 minutes.

16. Let cool on the baking sheets for 10 minutes before serving.

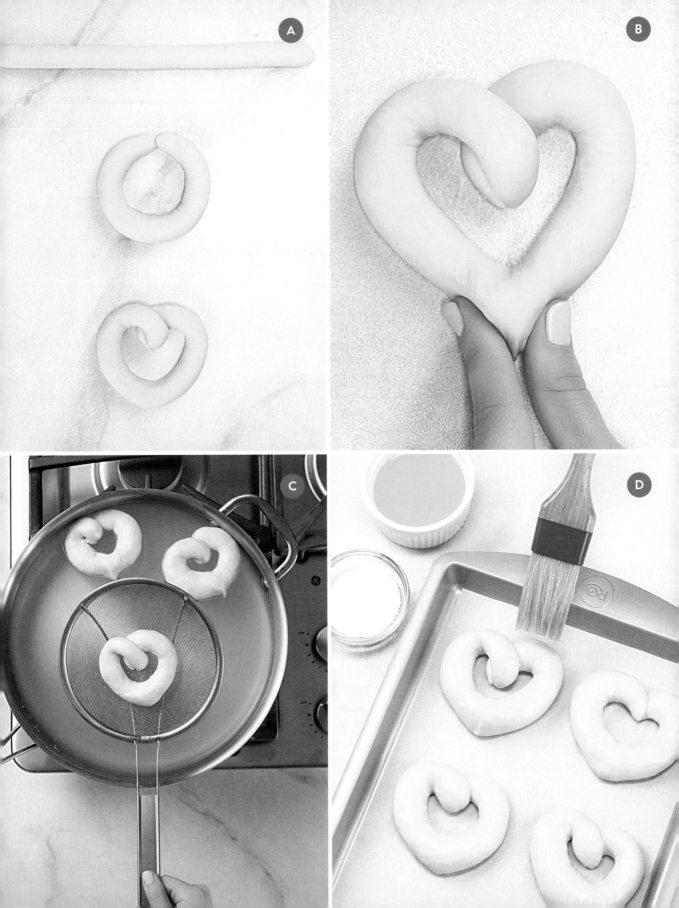

CHOCOLATE HEART
WHOOPIE PIES

My heart melts for chocolate. Especially for chocolate heart-shaped cookies sandwiching fluffy caramel frosting. These lovely desserts are the perfect way to celebrate Valentine's Day vegan style without compromising taste. Whoopie!

THE THINGS YOU'LL NEED

Vegan Chocolate Whoopie Cookie

⅔ cup unsweetened almond milk

½ teaspoon lemon juice

1½ cups all-purpose flour

5 tablespoons unsweetened cocoa powder

¾ teaspoon baking soda

¾ teaspoon baking powder

⅔ cup vegetable oil

½ cup granulated sugar

1 teaspoon vanilla extract

Caramel Filling

¾ cup Vegan Caramel Sauce (page 20)

8 tablespoons vegetable shortening

4 tablespoons vegan butter

1 teaspoon vanilla extract

3 to 4 cups powdered sugar

Equipment

2½-inch heart cookie cutter (template on page 248)

#12 decorating tip

LET'S GET STARTED!

1. Preheat the oven to 350°F. Line 2 baking sheets with parchment paper.
2. Make the chocolate whoopie cookie: In a small bowl, whisk together the almond milk and lemon juice. Allow the mixture to curdle, about 10 minutes.
3. In a medium bowl, whisk together the flour, cocoa powder, baking soda, and baking powder.
4. Whisk the oil, sugar, and 1 teaspoon vanilla into the curdled almond milk.
5. Make a well in the center of the flour mixture and pour in the wet mixture. Mix until well combined.
6. Place the heart cookie cutter on the prepared baking sheet and scoop 1 tablespoon of the batter into the center. Spread evenly, then remove the cookie cutter. Repeat with the remaining batter.
7. Bake until the edges are set and the top is soft to the touch, 10 to 12 minutes.
8. Let cool on the baking sheets for 5 minutes, then transfer to a wire rack to cool completely.
9. Make the caramel filling: Make the Vegan Caramel Sauce and transfer to a large bowl. Add the shortening, vegan butter, and 1 teaspoon vanilla and beat with an electric mixer until creamy. Add the powdered sugar ½ cup at a time, beating well after each addition, until the filling is stiff enough to pipe (you may not need to use all the sugar).
10. Scoop the filling into a piping bag fitted with a #12 decorating tip.
11. Turn half the hearts upside down and pipe filling onto the flat side. Top with the remaining hearts, flat side down.

HEART
RAVIOLI

Making handmade pasta is a long-standing tradition in my family that I truly enjoy. We cherish getting together on holidays to cook up new memories and good food. This recipe is perfect for a romantic date night. It's simple, adorable, and tasty.

THE THINGS YOU'LL NEED

Pasta Dough
2 cups all-purpose flour
½ teaspoon salt
3 large eggs
2 tablespoons olive oil
3 tablespoons water

Cheese Filling
1 cup ricotta cheese
½ cup grated Parmesan cheese
½ cup shredded mozzarella cheese
¼ teaspoon freshly ground pepper
¼ teaspoon salt
½ teaspoon grated lemon zest
¼ teaspoon garlic powder

Marinara Sauce
1 tablespoon olive oil
8 cloves garlic, minced
1 small yellow onion, finely diced
1 can (28 ounces) crushed
    tomatoes
1 tablespoon tomato paste
1 cup vegetable stock
½ teaspoon Italian seasoning
1 teaspoon salt
½ teaspoon freshly ground pepper
½ teaspoon sugar

Equipment
Stand mixer fitted with the dough
    hook
Pasta roller
2½-inch heart cookie cutter
    (template on page 248)

LET'S GET STARTED!

1. Make the pasta dough: In a stand mixer fitted with the dough hook, mix together the flour and salt.
2. Make three small holes in the flour mixture and place an egg in each. On low speed, mix until a coarse meal forms.
3. With the mixer running, drizzle in the olive oil and add the water. Mix until a dough starts to form.
4. Turn the dough out onto a lightly floured surface and knead until smooth.
5. Wrap the dough in plastic wrap and let rest at room temperature for 30 minutes.
6. Make the cheese filling: In a medium bowl, mix together the ricotta, Parmesan, mozzarella, pepper, salt, lemon zest, and garlic powder until well combined.
7. Make the marinara sauce: In a large sauté pan, heat the olive oil over medium heat. Add the garlic and onion and sauté until translucent, 3 to 5 minutes. Reduce the heat and stir in the crushed tomatoes, tomato paste, vegetable stock, Italian seasoning, salt, pepper, and sugar. Let simmer, stirring occasionally, until the sauce thickens slightly, 10 to 15 minutes. Warm before using.
8. Assemble the ravioli: Line a baking sheet with parchment paper and lightly dust with flour.
9. On a floured surface, divide the pasta dough into 8 portions. Cover with a clean cloth to prevent a skin from forming. Pass each portion through a pasta roller until 1/16 inch thick. Cover the rolled pasta sheets as you work to keep them from drying out.

• CONTINUES •

10. Lay a pasta sheet on your work surface. Scoop 2 teaspoons of filling 1½ inches apart staggered down the pasta sheet. Dab water around the filling with a finger (A). Place a second pasta sheet over the first and press the areas around the filling to seal (B).

11. Cut out ravioli using the heart cutter (C). Crimp the edges of the pasta together with a fork to seal (D). Place the ravioli on the baking sheet as you finish them. Repeat with the remaining pasta sheets and filling.

12. Bring a large pot of salted water to a boil. Add the ravioli and cook until they float to the top, 2 to 4 minutes. Drain the ravioli and gently toss with olive oil.

13. Serve with the marinara sauce, sliced fresh basil, and grated Parmesan.

CHAPTER TWO

EASTER

CHOCOLATE
BIRD NEST COOKIES

—— MAKES 12 COOKIES ——

I'll never forget the first time I tried coconut and chocolate together. After this life-changing experience, I had to develop a recipe using the same flavor combination. With simple ingredients and only a few easy steps to follow, these cookies are definitely worth tweeting about. Even better, they are completely gluten-free.

THE THINGS YOU'LL NEED

Chocolate Cookie

7 ounces dark chocolate, chopped
3 large egg whites
⅔ cup sugar
¼ cup unsweetened cocoa powder
¼ teaspoon salt
1 teaspoon vanilla extract
2½ cups sweetened shredded
    coconut

Decorations

1 batch Royal Icing (page 16)
Food coloring: black and orange
36 mini candy eggs (Cadbury)
Check the label to be sure the candy eggs are manufactured in a gluten-free environment.

Equipment

Two #1 decorating tips

LET'S GET STARTED!

1. Preheat the oven to 350°F. Line a baking sheet with parchment paper.
2. Melt the dark chocolate.
3. In a large bowl, whisk together the egg whites and sugar until frothy. Whisk in the cocoa powder, salt, and vanilla.
4. Using a spatula fold in the melted chocolate and coconut until well combined.
5. Shape 2 tablespoons of batter into a nest. Place 1 inch apart on the baking sheet.
6. Bake until the cookies are firm to the touch, 12 to 15 minutes.
7. Let cool on the baking sheet for 2 minutes, then transfer to a wire rack to cool completely.

TIME TO DECORATE!

1. Make the Royal Icing. Divide it between 2 bowls and tint one bowl black and the other orange. Scoop into separate decorating bags fitted with #1 tips.
2. Pipe 2 black dots on the candy eggs for eyes. Pipe a small orange triangle for the beak.
3. Place 3 eggs in each nest.

CARROT CAKE

My mother's favorite type of cake is carrot cake. Some of my fondest memories are helping her bake this dessert to serve after Easter dinner. It's a perfectly spiced cake recipe made with fresh shredded carrots and topped with a heavenly cream cheese frosting.

THE THINGS YOU'LL NEED

Carrot Cake
3½ cups all-purpose flour
4 cups packed dark brown sugar
4 teaspoons ground cinnamon
¼ teaspoon ground nutmeg
1 tablespoon baking powder
1 teaspoon baking soda
1½ teaspoons salt
3 sticks (12 ounces) unsalted butter, melted
4 large eggs
2 teaspoons vanilla extract
6 cups shredded carrots

Decorations
2 batches Cream Cheese Frosting (page 18)
Food coloring: green and orange

Equipment
Decorating tips: #5, #32

LET'S GET STARTED!

1. Preheat the oven to 350°F. Grease two 8-inch round cake pans and line the bottoms with rounds of parchment paper.
2. In a large bowl, mix together the flour, brown sugar, cinnamon, nutmeg, baking powder, baking soda, and salt.
3. In a medium bowl, whisk together the melted butter, eggs, and vanilla.
4. Make a well in the center of the flour mixture and add the wet mixture. Mix until no dry streaks of flour remain (do not overmix).
5. Fold in the shredded carrots.
6. Divide the batter evenly between the prepared pans and bake until a wooden pick inserted into the center comes out clean, 45 to 55 minutes.
7. Let cool in the pans for 15 minutes, then turn out onto a wire rack to cool completely.
8. Level off the tops with a cake leveler or a large serrated knife.

TIME TO DECORATE!

1. Make the Cream Cheese Frosting. Tint one-quarter of the frosting green and scoop into a decorating bag fitted with a #32 tip.
2. Tint the remaining frosting orange. Scoop a small amount into a decorating bag fitted with a #5 tip.
3. Stack the cakes with a thin layer of orange frosting in between them. Frost the entire cake with the orange frosting.
4. Pipe an orange outline around the top edge of the cake. Pipe lines to create 12 equal-size carrot-shaped wedges. Pipe 3 diagonal lines inside each triangle for carrot details.
5. Pipe green frosting shells at the end of each triangle for the carrot tops.

BUNNY BUM
CAKE BALLS

MAKES 20 CAKE BALLS

Have a Hoppy Easter! These adorable bite-size bunny bums will easily make your loved ones smile and are a cute treat to share for brunch. This recipe creates white chocolate covered strawberry cake balls that have all the flavor of a chocolate-dipped strawberry. They are so yummy there won't be any left behind.

THE THINGS YOU'LL NEED

Strawberry Cake
10 large strawberries, cut into
   ¼-inch-thick slices
1 tablespoon plus ¾ cup sugar
1 tablespoon plus 1½ teaspoons
   water
1½ teaspoons cornstarch
1 cup all-purpose flour
1 teaspoon baking powder
½ teaspoon salt
4 tablespoons unsalted butter, at
   room temperature
2 large egg whites
½ teaspoon vanilla extract
½ cup whole milk

Decorations
2 bags (12 ounces each) bright
   white Candy Melts (Wilton) or
   white chocolate
1 bag (12 ounces) pink Candy Melts
   (Wilton)
10 mini marshmallows (Jet-Puffed)
White nonpareils

Equipment
Stand mixer fitted with the paddle
   attachment
 Bunny feet template (page 248)
Decorating tips: #2, #3

LET'S GET STARTED!

1. Preheat the oven to 350°F. Grease an 8 x 8-inch metal baking pan and line the bottom with parchment paper.
2. In a small saucepan, combine the strawberries, the 1 tablespoon sugar, and 1 tablespoon water and bring to a boil, stirring occasionally.
3. In a small bowl, whisk together the cornstarch and the 1½ teaspoons water. Add the mixture to the saucepan and stir constantly until thickened, 2 to 3 minutes. Remove from the heat and let cool.
4. In a medium bowl, whisk together the flour, baking powder, and salt.
5. In a large bowl, with an electric mixer, beat the butter and the ¾ cup sugar until light and fluffy, 3 to 5 minutes.
6. Add the egg whites to the butter mixture one at a time, mixing after each addition.
7. Mix in the vanilla and the cooled strawberry mixture.
8. On low speed, alternate adding the flour mixture and the milk to the butter mixture, beginning and ending with the flour mixture.
9. Pour the batter into the prepared pan and bake until a wooden pick inserted into the center comes out clean, 25 to 30 minutes.
10. Let cool in the pan for 15 minutes, then turn out onto a wire rack to cool completely.
11. In the bowl of a stand mixer, break the cake into pieces. Fit the mixer with the paddle attachment. On low speed, beat until a dough-like mixture forms, 3 to 5 minutes.

• CONTINUES •

12. Line a baking sheet with wax paper. Roll 1½ tablespoons of dough into a ball and place on the baking sheet. Repeat to make about 20 cake balls.
13. Refrigerate the cake balls until firm, about 1 hour.

TIME TO DECORATE!

1. Melt 1 bag of the white Candy Melts. Dip the cake balls into the melted candy with a fork, letting the excess candy drip off. Place back on the baking sheet **A**.
2. To make the bunny feet, place the bunny feet template on a second baking sheet and lay wax paper over the template.
3. Melt the remaining bag of white Candy Melts. Scoop the melted candy into a decorating bag fitted with a #3 tip and pipe the bunny feet onto the wax paper following the template **B**. Each cake ball needs 2 bunny feet, for a total of 40. Let harden for 10 minutes, then flip the feet over.
4. Melt the pink Candy Melts. Scoop into a decorating bag fitted with a #2 tip and pipe pink paw print details on the flat side of each foot **C**.
5. To make the bunny tails, cut each mini marshmallow in half. Shape into balls, then roll in white nonpareils to coat **D**.
6. Using melted white candy, attach the feet and tails to the cake balls.

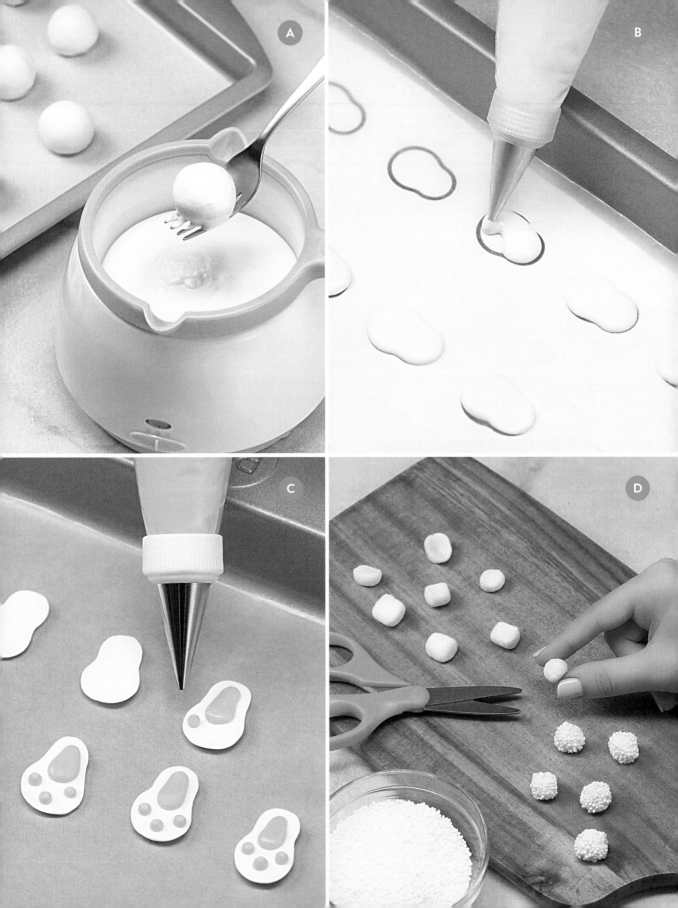

MINI EASTER EGG
CUPCAKES

Easter brings back a lot of fun memories for me. Growing up, my sister and I would always wake up early, excited for the annual Easter egg hunt. We loved running around the house looking for hidden jelly bean–filled eggs. The Easter Bunny often included vegan and dairy-free candy because my sister is lactose intolerant. How thoughtful. This recipe is inspired by our family tradition, which has continued throughout the years. They're vegan, dairy-free, and taste Eggcellent!

THE THINGS YOU'LL NEED

Vegan Chocolate Cake
1½ cups all-purpose flour
¼ cup unsweetened cocoa powder
1 tablespoon baking soda
½ cup granulated sugar
½ cup coconut sugar
½ teaspoon sea salt
¼ cup coconut oil, melted
1½ tablespoons distilled white
   vinegar
1 teaspoon vanilla extract
1 cup water

Decorations
1 batch Vegan Buttercream
   Frosting (page 17)
Vegan green food coloring
Vegan jelly beans (Brach's)

Equipment
#233 decorating tip

LET'S GET STARTED!

1. Preheat the oven to 350°F. Line a mini muffin tin with mini brown paper liners.
2. In a large bowl, whisk together the flour, cocoa powder, baking soda, granulated sugar, coconut sugar, and sea salt.
3. In a medium bowl, whisk together the coconut oil, vinegar, vanilla, and water.
4. Make a well in the center of the flour mixture and add the wet mixture. Stir until no dry streaks of flour remain (do not overmix).
5. Fill the paper liners two-thirds full with batter. Bake until a wooden pick inserted into the center of a cupcake comes out clean, 14 to 16 minutes.
6. Transfer to a wire rack to cool.

TIME TO DECORATE!

1. Make the Vegan Buttercream Frosting. Tint green and scoop into a decorating bag fitted with a #233 tip. Pipe grass to cover the top of the cooled cupcakes.
2. Place 3 jelly beans in the center of each cupcake.

CHICK CRINKLE COOKIES

— MAKES ABOUT 20 COOKIES —

Spring has sprung! These adorable baby chicks put a fun twist on a traditionally wintertime cookie. Crinkle Cookies are one of my favorites, especially when they're made from scratch using fresh lemons from my backyard. The lemon flavor makes these a fantastically refreshing dessert. While they're almost too cute to eat, you'll be happy you gave them a try.

THE THINGS YOU'LL NEED

Lemon Cookies

1¾ cups all-purpose flour
½ teaspoon salt
¼ teaspoon baking powder
⅛ teaspoon baking soda
8 tablespoons (1 stick) unsalted butter, at room temperature
¾ cup granulated sugar
1 large egg
1 tablespoon grated lemon zest
2 tablespoons lemon juice
¼ teaspoon lemon yellow food coloring gel

Coating

2 cups powdered sugar, sifted
1 cup granulated sugar

Decorations

1 batch Royal Icing (page 16)
Food coloring: black and orange

Equipment

Two #1 decorating tips

LET'S GET STARTED!

1. Make the lemon cookies: In a medium bowl, whisk together the flour, salt, baking powder, and baking soda.
2. In a large bowl, with an electric mixer, beat the butter and ¾ cup granulated sugar until light and fluffy, 3 to 5 minutes. Add the egg and beat well.
3. Beat in the lemon zest, lemon juice, and yellow food coloring until well combined. On low speed, slowly beat in the flour mixture until combined.
4. Cover the bowl with plastic wrap and refrigerate for 1 hour.
5. Preheat the oven to 350°F. Line a baking sheet with parchment paper.
6. Roll the chilled dough into 1-tablespoon balls.

• CONTINUES •

7. Coat the cookies: For the chick body, roll two-thirds of the balls in the powdered sugar and place 2 inches apart on the baking sheet (A).

8. For the chick head, roll the remaining balls in the granulated sugar. Cut each ball in half (B) and place the cut side against a powdered sugar cookie ball on the baking sheet (C).

9. Bake until set but not browned at the edges, 10 to 12 minutes.

10. Let cool on the baking sheet for 2 minutes, then transfer to a wire rack to cool completely.

TIME TO DECORATE!

1. Make the Royal Icing. Divide it between 2 bowls and tint one bowl black and the other orange. Scoop the icings into separate decorating bags fitted with #1 tips.

2. Pipe 2 black dots on the "head" cookie for eyes.

3. Pipe an upside-down orange triangle for the beak. Pipe 2 orange feet at the bottom of the "body" cookie (D).

MOTHER'S DAY

ROSÉ MUG CAKE

My mom is one of the sweetest and happiest people I've ever met in my life. When Mother's Day comes around, I can't wait to bake something for her to show my appreciation. On special occasions, she loves to have a glass of wine, so we make sure to stop and smell the rosé. This cake recipe is made in a similar way to mug cakes, which means they are quick, easy, and only need to cook for about a minute in the microwave.

THE THINGS YOU'LL NEED

Rosé Syrup
6 tablespoons sparkling rosé wine
5 tablespoons granulated sugar

Rosé Cake
6 tablespoons cake flour, sifted
1 tablespoon powdered sugar, sifted
½ teaspoon baking powder
½ teaspoon salt
½ cup whole milk
1 tablespoon vegetable oil
½ teaspoon vanilla extract
Pink food coloring

Rosé Frosting
⅓ cup heavy cream
1 tablespoon rosé syrup
2 teaspoons powdered sugar
Pink food coloring

Decorations
2 teaspoons edible light pink sugar
    pearls

Equipment
2 coupe champagne glasses
    (5.25 ounces)
#824 decorating tip

LET'S GET STARTED!

1. Make the rosé syrup: In a heatproof bowl, mix the sparkling wine and granulated sugar. Microwave in 1-minute increments, stirring after each, until thickened but still pink, 3 to 4 minutes. Let cool to room temperature.
2. Make the rosé cake: In a small bowl, mix the cake flour, powdered sugar, baking powder, and salt.
3. Whisk in the milk, ¼ cup of the rosé syrup, oil, and vanilla. Tint with pink food coloring and whisk until combined.
4. Lightly grease two 5.25-ounce champagne coupes. Divide the batter evenly between the glasses.
5. Microwave the glasses one at a time until baked, 60 to 90 seconds.
6. Allow the cakes to cool.

TIME TO DECORATE!

1. Make the rosé frosting: In a medium bowl, with an electric mixer, beat the heavy cream, rosé syrup, powdered sugar, and pink food coloring until medium peaks form.
2. Scoop the frosting into a decorating bag fitted with a #824 tip.
3. Pipe a swirl of rosé frosting onto each cake.
4. Top with light pink pearls.

BAKED CREAM
CREPES

──── MAKES 12 CREPES ────

Growing up, I loved making my mom breakfast in bed for Mother's Day. It was my way of making her morning extra special and showing my gratitude for everything she does. Not only are these crepes a great recipe but they also make a thoughtful gift.

THE THINGS YOU'LL NEED

Cream Filling

1 package (8 ounces) cream cheese, at room temperature
1 cup mascarpone cheese
1 tablespoon grated lemon zest
Seeds of ½ vanilla bean
2 tablespoons sugar

Crepes

1½ cups whole milk
3 tablespoons unsalted butter, melted
2 large eggs
½ teaspoon vanilla extract
¼ teaspoon almond extract
¼ cup sugar
¼ teaspoon salt
1 cup all-purpose flour

For Assembly

4 tablespoons unsalted butter, melted
¼ cup sugar

Decorations

12 large strawberries
1 cup blueberries
1 cup raspberries
½ cup blackberries

Equipment

9 x 13-inch baking dish
1-inch heart cookie cutter

LET'S GET STARTED!

1. Make the cream filling: In a large bowl, with an electric mixer, beat the cream cheese, mascarpone cheese, lemon zest, vanilla seeds, and sugar until smooth.
2. Make the crepes: In a blender, mix the milk, 3 tablespoons melted butter, eggs, vanilla, almond extract, sugar, and salt.
3. Add the flour and blend until smooth. Allow the batter to sit for 10 minutes.
4. Preheat the oven to 375°F.
5. Grease a medium skillet with cooking spray and heat over medium-low heat. Pour ¼ cup of batter in and swirl the pan to make sure the batter coats the entire surface. Cook for about 1 minute, then flip the crepe and cook the other side, about 30 seconds. Repeat with the remaining batter.
6. To assemble, brush the bottom of a 9 x 13-inch baking dish with half the melted butter and sprinkle with half the sugar.
7. Scoop 2½ tablespoons of filling into the center of a crepe. Fold the crepe sides in, then pull up the bottom and flip the crepe over to seal in the filling. Place the filled crepes in the baking dish.
8. Brush the tops of the crepes with the remaining melted butter and sprinkle with the remaining sugar.
9. Bake until lightly browned, about 14 minutes.

TIME TO DECORATE!

1. Slice the strawberries and use the mini heart cookie cutter to cut the slices into hearts.
2. Top the crepes with the strawberry hearts, blueberries, raspberries, and blackberries.

ROSE CUPCAKE BOUQUET

I made this Rose Cupcake Bouquet one year for my mom and it was a big hit. It's one of my most requested baked gift ideas and is a great alternative to giving traditional roses. This is also something I've started to re-create often throughout the year for holidays such as birthdays, weddings, Valentine's Day, and more. It makes a beautiful centerpiece and is an after-dinner dessert for the whole family to share.

THE THINGS YOU'LL NEED

White Chocolate Raspberry Cake
1½ cups all-purpose flour
½ teaspoon baking powder
¼ teaspoon baking soda
½ teaspoon salt
8 tablespoons (1 stick) unsalted
    butter, at room temperature
¾ cup sugar
3 large eggs
½ teaspoon almond extract
½ cup sour cream
1 cup white chocolate chips
    (Nestlé)
1 cup frozen raspberries

Decorations
1 batch Swiss Buttercream Frosting
    (page 17)
Pink food coloring

Equipment
Green paper cupcake liners
#2D decorating tip
6-inch-diameter foam sphere
6-inch-diameter ceramic pot
Toothpicks
2½-inch green tissue paper squares

LET'S GET STARTED!

1. Preheat the oven to 325°F. Line 16 cups of 2 muffin tins with paper liners.
2. In a medium bowl, whisk together the flour, baking powder, baking soda, and salt.
3. In a large bowl, with an electric mixer, beat the butter and sugar until light and fluffy, 3 to 5 minutes.
4. Add the eggs one at a time, beating well after each addition.
5. Beat in the almond extract.
6. On low speed, alternate adding the flour mixture and the sour cream to the butter mixture, beginning and ending with the flour mixture.
7. With a spatula, fold in the white chocolate chips and raspberries.
8. Fill each paper liner two-thirds full with batter and bake until a wooden pick inserted into the center of a cupcake comes out clean, about 24 minutes.
9. Transfer to a wire rack to cool.

TIME TO DECORATE!

1. Make the Swiss Buttercream Frosting. Tint pink and scoop into a decorating bag fitted with a #2D tip.

• CONTINUES •

2. Pipe a flat rose on top of each cupcake (A). Refrigerate the cupcakes for 10 to 15 minutes to firm the cupcakes and set the frosting.

3. Place the foam sphere in the ceramic pot, making sure it fits securely.

4. Place 13 sets of 2 toothpicks all around the foam ball (tilted upward slightly), leaving 1½ inches clear above the rim of the pot (B).

5. Attach the cupcakes to the toothpicks (C).

6. Overlap 2 tissue paper squares, then gather the center and pack tightly between the cupcakes (D).

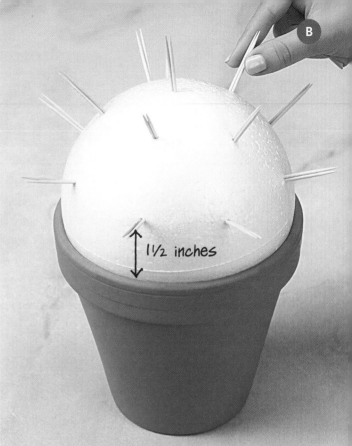

1½ inches

DAISY LEMON TARTS

When I was a little girl, I loved making daisy chains and crowns with my mom and sister in our backyard. We would picnic in the grass for hours and laugh about everything. I can't help but be reminded of these wonderful memories every time I see daisies. Daisies are my mom's favorite flower and this recipe is inspired by them.

THE THINGS YOU'LL NEED

Tart Dough
2 large egg yolks
2 tablespoons heavy cream
½ teaspoon lemon extract
1½ cups all-purpose flour
8 tablespoons (1 stick) unsalted butter, cut into cubes and chilled
¼ cup granulated sugar
¼ teaspoon salt

Lemon Curd Filling
1 large egg
2 large egg yolks
½ cup granulated sugar
Grated zest of 1 large lemon
¼ cup lemon juice
4 tablespoons unsalted butter, at room temperature

Decoration
¼ cup powdered sugar

Equipment
Stand mixer fitted with the paddle attachment
Two 12-cup mini muffin tins
Flower cookie cutter (template on page 248)

LET'S GET STARTED!

1. Make the tart dough: In small bowl, whisk together the egg yolks, heavy cream, and lemon extract until smooth.
2. In a stand mixer fitted with the paddle attachment, mix the flour, butter, ¼ cup granulated sugar, and salt on low speed until a coarse meal forms.
3. On low speed, slowly mix in the cream mixture until the dough holds together when pinched.
4. Shape the dough into a disk and wrap with plastic wrap. Refrigerate for 1 hour.
5. Make the lemon curd filling: Fill a small saucepan halfway with warm water and bring to a simmer.

• CONTINUES •

6. In a heatproof bowl (that fits over the saucepan), whisk the egg, egg yolks, ½ cup granulated sugar, lemon zest, and lemon juice. Place the bowl over the saucepan, making sure the bottom of the bowl isn't touching the simmering water. Whisk occasionally, until the mixture thickens, 8 to 10 minutes **A**.

7. Strain the mixture through a fine-mesh sieve set over a medium bowl. Stir in the butter until melted and fully combined.

8. Lay a piece of plastic wrap against the top of the filling so that a skin does not form **B**. Set aside to cool, about 1 hour.

9. Preheat the oven to 350°F. Grease 12 cups of the mini muffin tins, greasing every other cup.

10. On a lightly floured surface, roll out the dough to a ¼-inch thickness. Cut out 12 tart shells using the flower cookie cutter.

11. Press the center of the flowers into the greased mini muffin cups. The petals of the flower will hang around the edges of the cup. Use a fork to dock the bottom of the tart shells **C**.

12. Freeze for 10 to 15 minutes to firm up the dough.

13. Bake until firm to the touch, 10 to 12 minutes.

14. Let cool in the pans on a wire rack.

TIME TO DECORATE!

1. Using a sifter, cover each tart shell with powdered sugar.

2. Fill each tart with lemon curd filling **D**.

WINE GUMMY BEARS

What could possibly be better than delicious gummy bears? Delicious gummy bears infused with wine! My mom and I recently discovered champagne gummy bears at a local boutique shop in Los Angeles and we immediately fell in love with them. So, I thought it would be fun to expand these flavors to include red, white, and rosé wine.

THE THINGS YOU'LL NEED

Wine Gummy Bears

3 envelopes (¼ ounce each) unflavored gelatin

¼ cup plus ⅓ cup wine of your choice (red, white, or rosé)

½ cup sugar

2 tablespoons light corn syrup

¾ teaspoon citric acid

Equipment

Squeeze bottle or dropper

Gummy bear molds (Ro Baking Line by Wilton)

LET'S GET STARTED!

1. In a small bowl, mix together the gelatin and ¼ cup of the wine. Set aside to bloom until grainy and firm, 3 to 5 minutes.

2. In a small saucepan, mix together the sugar, corn syrup, and remaining ⅓ cup wine and bring to a boil over medium heat. Reduce the heat and simmer for 10 minutes.

3. Remove from the heat and whisk in the gelatin mixture and citric acid until completely dissolved.

4. Strain the mixture through a fine-mesh sieve set over a medium bowl.

5. Using a dropper, carefully fill each mold cavity.

6. Refrigerate until set, 1 to 2 hours.

7. Line a baking sheet with parchment paper. Once the gummy bears are completely set, pop them out of the molds and place them on the baking sheet. Let sit at room temperature for 24 hours to form a skin.

LOVE IS LIKE
WINE,
IT GETS BETTER
WITH TIME.

FATHER'S DAY

MUSTACHE DONUTS

MAKES 10 TO 12 MUSTACHES

Fun fact: My dad has had an awesome mustache since the seventh grade. I have never seen him without it. It's iconic and deserves its own themed treat!

THE THINGS YOU'LL NEED

Donuts

1 envelope (¼ ounce) active dry yeast
¾ cup warm milk
3 tablespoons granulated sugar
Seeds of ½ vanilla bean
¼ teaspoon almond extract
2 large egg yolks
2 tablespoons unsalted butter, at room temperature
2½ to 3 cups all-purpose flour
¼ teaspoon salt
1 tablespoon oil, for coating the bowl and dough
About 8 cups vegetable oil, for deep-frying

Frosting

2 cups powdered sugar
½ cup unsweetened cocoa powder
7 tablespoons hot water
½ cup chocolate chips

Equipment

Stand mixer fitted with the dough hook
Large heavy-bottomed pot
Candy thermometer
Mustache cookie cutter (Ro Baking Line by Wilton, or template on page 248)
#4 decorating tip

LET'S GET STARTED!

1. Make the donuts: In the bowl of a stand mixer, whisk together the yeast, warm milk, and granulated sugar. Set aside until foamy, about 10 minutes.
2. Stir in the vanilla seeds, almond extract, egg yolks, and butter.
3. Stir ½ cup of the flour into the yeast mixture until a thick paste forms.
4. On low speed, beat in the salt and the remaining flour, ¼ cup at a time. Mix until the dough is soft and pulls away from the sides of the bowl (you may not need to use all the flour), 3 to 5 minutes.
5. On a lightly floured surface knead the dough for 1 minute. Form the dough into a large ball. If the dough is too sticky, add more flour as needed.
6. Grease a large bowl with the oil and add the dough. Roll the dough in the oil to completely coat. Cover the bowl with a clean cloth and let rest at room temperature until doubled in size, 1 to 2 hours.
7. Pour about 4 inches of vegetable oil into a large heavy-bottomed pot fitted with a candy thermometer. Heat the oil to 350°F over medium heat. Line a baking sheet with parchment paper.
8. On a lightly floured surface, flatten the dough to ½ inch thick.
9. Cut out donuts with the mustache cookie cutter and place on the baking sheet. Cover with a clean cloth so a skin does not form and let rest for 10 to 15 minutes.
10. Working in batches of a few at a time, fry the donuts until golden brown, 1 to 2 minutes per side. Remove with a slotted spoon and let drain on paper towels.

TIME TO DECORATE!

1. Make the frosting: In a large bowl, with an electric mixer, beat the powdered sugar, cocoa powder, and hot water.
2. Melt the chocolate and beat into the powdered sugar mixture until smooth.
3. Scoop the frosting into a decorating bag fitted with a #4 tip.
4. Use the frosting to outline the donuts. Fill in the center and let dry 5 minutes.
5. Pipe mustache details.

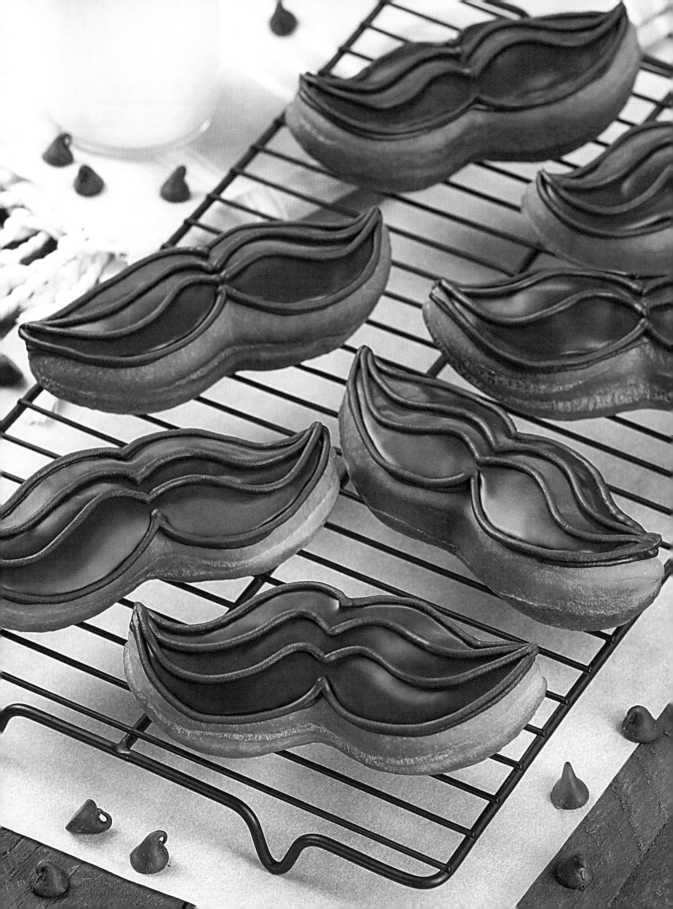

SALTED WHISKEY CARAMELS

MAKES 4 TO 5 DOZEN CARAMELS

When our family took a trip to Ireland, one of the first things my dad wanted to do was go whiskey tasting. It's such a passion for him that he even distills his own custom whiskey. I have tried many caramel recipes over the years and this one is hands down my favorite. These tasty bite-size candies are soft and smooth with a hint of salt.

THE THINGS YOU'LL NEED

Salted Whiskey Caramels

8 tablespoons (1 stick) unsalted butter
½ cup plus 2 tablespoons sweetened condensed milk
½ cup packed light brown sugar
½ cup packed dark brown sugar
¼ cup honey
¼ cup corn syrup
1 tablespoon bourbon extract
¼ cup Irish whiskey (Jameson)
Sea salt, for topping

Equipment

Medium heavy-bottomed stainless-steel saucepan (do not use a nonstick pan)
Candy thermometer
3-inch wax paper squares, for wrapping

LET'S GET STARTED!

1. Grease an 8 x 8-inch metal baking pan and line the bottom and two sides of the pan with parchment paper (leave an overhang to make it easier to take out of the pan). Grease the paper.
2. In a heavy-bottomed saucepan fitted with a candy thermometer, combine the butter, condensed milk, light brown sugar, dark brown sugar, honey, corn syrup, bourbon extract, and whiskey.
3. Set the saucepan over medium heat and bring to 250°F, mixing with a heat-resistant spatula every few minutes.
4. Pour the caramel mixture into the prepared pan and let cool for 30 minutes. Sprinkle with sea salt.
5. Let sit at room temperature until firm, 4 to 6 hours.
6. Remove the caramel from the pan. Cut into 1-inch squares.
7. Wrap each caramel with wax paper and store in an airtight container.

‹ RO TIP ›

To make this recipe ALCOHOL-FREE, replace the whiskey with WATER and the bourbon extract with VANILLA EXTRACT.

Mom and Dad making whiskey

BBQ GRILL CUPCAKES

MAKES 20 BROWNIE CUPCAKES

If there's one thing I know about my dad, it's that he loves to grill. For as long as I can remember, he would invite friends and family over on the weekends for fun outdoor get-togethers. These grill cupcakes feature candy versions of some backyard classics.

THE THINGS YOU'LL NEED

Brownie Cupcakes
¾ cup all-purpose flour
2 tablespoons unsweetened cocoa powder
½ teaspoon baking powder
½ teaspoon salt
8 tablespoons (1 stick) unsalted butter
4 ounces dark chocolate, chopped
4 large eggs
¾ cup granulated sugar
1½ teaspoons vanilla extract
¼ cup water

Decorations
Orange sanding sugar
1 batch Royal Icing (page 16)
Black food coloring
Colorful fruit gummies (gummy bears)
Red oblong fruit chews (Hot Tamales)
Black FoodWriter pen (Wilton)
Soft caramel candies (Kraft)
White candy–coated black licorice (Good & Plenty)
Chocolate candy rolls (Tootsie Roll)
Yellow taffy (Laffy Taffy, banana)

Equipment
#3 decorating tip
Toothpicks

LET'S GET STARTED!

1. Preheat the oven to 325ºF. Line 2 muffin tins with brown paper liners.
2. In a small bowl, whisk together the flour, cocoa powder, baking powder, and salt.
3. Melt the butter and chocolate together. Let cool slightly.
4. In a large bowl, with an electric mixer, beat together the eggs, granulated sugar, and vanilla until doubled in volume and light in color, about 10 minutes.
5. On low speed, slowly add the chocolate-butter mixture to the egg mixture and mix until fully combined.
6. Slowly mix in the water.
7. Fold in one-third of the flour mixture just until no dry streaks remain (do not overmix). Repeat two more times.
8. Fill each paper liner two-thirds full with batter and bake until a wooden pick inserted into the center of a cupcake comes out clean, about 20 minutes.
9. Transfer to a wire rack to cool.

TIME TO DECORATE!

1. Sprinkle orange sanding sugar on top of the cupcakes to look like fire embers.
2. Make the Royal Icing. Tint with black food coloring until you reach the desired shade of gray and scoop the icing into a decorating bag fitted with a #3 tip.
3. Pipe grill grates on top of the cupcakes. Allow to dry.
4. To make kebabs, cut the gummy bears into slices and slide onto toothpicks.
5. To make hot dogs, draw grill marks on the Hot Tamales using a black FoodWriter pen.
6. To make steaks, form a caramel into a steak shape and insert a white Good & Plenty for the bone. Draw grill marks on the caramels using the black FoodWriter pen.
7. To make cheeseburgers, cut the Tootsie Rolls into round slices for the patties. Mold the Laffy Taffy into cheese slices.
8. Place the candy decorations on top of the grills.

BASEBALL PIZZA

This traditional pizza recipe is a home run! Baseball has always been an important part of my dad's life. He used to coach my sister's little league team and enjoys taking our family to baseball games. We even have family pizza nights once a week, which has earned my dad the nickname "Papa Pizza."

THE THINGS YOU'LL NEED

Pizza Dough
2½ cups bread flour
1 envelope (¼ ounce) active dry
  yeast
1 teaspoon sugar
1 tablespoon salt
1¼ cups warm water
2 tablespoons extra virgin olive oil
1 tablespoon olive oil, for coating
  the bowl and the dough

Pizza Sauce (makes 1 cup)
¼ cup roasted garlic
½ cup tomato sauce
⅓ cup tomato paste
¼ cup water
1½ teaspoons chopped fresh basil
¼ teaspoon chopped fresh oregano
¼ teaspoon chopped fresh thyme
½ teaspoon sugar
¼ teaspoon salt
⅛ teaspoon freshly ground pepper

Decorations
1 cup coarse cornmeal
3 cups shredded mozzarella cheese
2 red bell peppers, sliced into short
  strips

Equipment
Pizza stone
Pizza peel or baking sheet

LET'S GET STARTED!

1. Make the pizza dough: In a large bowl, with a wooden spoon, mix the bread flour, yeast, sugar, and salt.
2. In a small bowl, mix the warm water and 2 tablespoons extra virgin olive oil.
3. Pour half the water-oil mixture into the flour mixture and mix with a wooden spoon until a thick paste forms. Add the remaining water-oil mixture and stir until a soft and sticky dough forms.
4. Grease a large bowl with the 1 tablespoon olive oil and place the dough inside. Turn to coat the dough. Cover the bowl with a clean cloth and let the dough rest at room temperature until doubled in size, 5 to 6 hours.
5. Make the sauce: In a small saucepan, whisk together the roasted garlic, tomato sauce, tomato paste, water, basil, oregano, thyme, sugar, salt, and pepper. Cook over low heat until slightly thickened, 10 to 15 minutes. Remove from the heat and set aside.

TIME TO DECORATE!

1. Position a rack in the upper third of the oven and place the pizza stone in the center of the rack. Preheat the oven to 500°F for 1 hour before baking the pizzas.
2. On a lightly floured surface, divide the dough into 3 portions. Roll each portion into a ball and cover with a clean cloth to prevent a skin from forming. Let rest for 15 minutes.
3. Sprinkle cornmeal onto a clean work surface. With damp hands, press each dough ball into a 10-inch round.
4. Sprinkle cornmeal on a pizza peel (or the back of a baking sheet) and slide one of the pizza crusts on top.
5. Spread one-third of the sauce over the crust and sprinkle evenly with 1 cup of the mozzarella.
6. Create a baseball stitch pattern with some of the red pepper strips.
7. Quickly slide the pizza onto the stone in the oven. Immediately turn the oven to broil for 2 to 3 minutes. Then turn the oven back to 500°F and bake until the cheese is melted and starting to brown, 2 to 3 minutes more. Repeat with the other 2 pizza crusts.

GERMAN CHOCOLATE STOUT
TRUFFLES

This recipe combines two of my dad's favorite things: German Chocolate Cake and Irish beer. He is half German and half Irish, which makes this the perfect gift for him on Father's Day. On the family trip to Ireland, my dad was beaming with excitement as we toured the factory where Guinness is made. After seeing how much he enjoyed it, I knew I had to create a custom treat for him. If your dad is anything like mine, he may love these.

THE THINGS YOU'LL NEED

German Chocolate Stout Truffles
½ cup sugar
1 teaspoon lemon juice
1 tablespoon water
¼ cup heavy cream
Seeds of ¼ vanilla bean
¼ teaspoon salt
¼ cup stout beer (Guinness)
1 tablespoon unsalted butter
9 ounces dark chocolate, chopped
½ cup sweetened shredded coconut

Decoration
2 cups ground pecans

Equipment
Medium heavy-bottomed stainless-steel saucepan (do not use a nonstick pan)
Candy thermometer

LET'S GET STARTED!

1. In a medium heavy-bottomed saucepan fitted with a candy thermometer, mix the sugar, lemon juice, and water. Set over medium heat and bring to 340°F, stirring constantly with a heat-resistant spatula.
2. Remove from the heat. Carefully whisk in the heavy cream. The mixture will bubble rapidly and steam.
3. Whisk in the vanilla seeds, salt, Guinness, and butter until combined.
4. Add 8 ounces of the chopped chocolate to the mixture and let melt, 1 to 3 minutes. Stir until smooth.
5. Fold in the coconut and remaining 1 ounce chocolate.
6. Pour into a heatproof container and refrigerate until set, 2 hours.

TIME TO DECORATE!

1. Put the ground pecans in a shallow bowl.
2. Scoop out 1 tablespoon of the chocolate truffle mixture and roll it into a ball, then roll in the ground pecans until fully covered. Repeat with the remaining truffle mixture.

RO TIP

To make this recipe ALCOHOL-FREE, use water instead of the stout.

CHAPTER FIVE

FOURTH OF JULY

STAR SCONES

MAKES 10 TO 12 SCONES

You guys, I have a confession to make. These scones are one of my favorite recipes in this book. I've made them for my family and friends many times in the past and they quickly disappear. If you want the best tasting get-together ever, start by baking a batch (or three) of them.

THE THINGS YOU'LL NEED

Berry Scones
4 large strawberries
½ cup blueberries
2 large egg yolks
½ cup heavy cream
1 teaspoon vanilla extract
3 cups all-purpose flour
½ cup granulated sugar
1 tablespoon baking powder
½ teaspoon salt
2 sticks (8 ounces) unsalted butter,
   cut into cubes and chilled

Topping
Heavy cream, for brushing
Granulated sugar, for sprinkling

Decorations
2 cups powdered sugar
3 tablespoons hot water

Equipment
Stand mixer fitted with the paddle
   attachment
3-inch star cookie cutter (template
   on page 248)

LET'S GET STARTED!

1. Preheat the oven to 350°F. Line a baking sheet with parchment paper.
2. Make the berry scones: Cut the strawberries into slices ⅛ inch thick and set aside with the blueberries.
3. In a small bowl, whisk together the egg yolks, ½ cup heavy cream, and vanilla.
4. In a stand mixer, on low speed, mix the flour, granulated sugar, baking powder, salt, and cubed butter until a coarse meal forms.
5. Slowly add the cream mixture until the dough holds together when pinched.
6. Using your hands, gently mix the blueberries and strawberry slices into the dough.
7. On a lightly floured surface, pat the dough out to a disk 1 inch thick.
8. Cut scones using the star cookie cutter and place the scones on the baking sheet, spacing them 2 inches apart. Dip the cutter in flour in between cuts.
9. Top the scones: Brush the scones with heavy cream and sprinkle with granulated sugar.
10. Bake until the scones turn golden brown at the points, 24 to 26 minutes.
11. Let cool on the baking sheet for 5 minutes, then transfer to a wire rack to cool completely.

TIME TO DECORATE!

1. In a small bowl, whisk together the powdered sugar and hot water until smooth.
2. Drizzle the icing over the scones.
3. Let the icing harden for 5 minutes before serving.

BLACKBERRY COBBLER

Growing up in Seattle there was never a shortage of blackberries flourishing in the wild. Next to my house was a park that had blackberry bushes everywhere. During the summer my mom and I would spend hours picking enough berries to fill several baskets to take home. We used them to make pies, jams, and cobblers. This is our family cobbler recipe and I love it berry much!

THE THINGS YOU'LL NEED

Blackberry Filling
6 cups blackberries
3 tablespoons honey
1 tablespoon cornstarch
½ teaspoon salt
Grated zest of 1 lemon

Cobbler Dough
1 cup heavy cream
¼ cup honey
1 cup all-purpose flour
¼ cup cornmeal
1½ teaspoons baking powder
½ teaspoon salt
½ teaspoon ground cinnamon

Topping
1 tablespoon heavy cream
2 teaspoons raw sugar

Equipment
2-quart baking dish

LET'S GET STARTED!

1. Preheat the oven to 350°F. Grease a 2-quart baking dish.
2. Make the blackberry filling: In a large bowl, gently toss the berries, honey, cornstarch, salt, and lemon zest. Place in the baking dish.
3. Make the cobbler dough: In a small bowl, mix together the heavy cream and honey.
4. In a medium bowl, whisk together the flour, cornmeal, baking powder, salt, and cinnamon.
5. Pour the cream mixture into the flour mixture and stir just until no dry streaks remain (do not overmix).
6. Scoop 2-tablespoon portions of dough onto the berry filling.
7. Top the cobbler: Brush the dough with the heavy cream and sprinkle with the raw sugar.
8. Bake until the fruit filling is bubbling and the topping is golden brown, 50 to 55 minutes.

STRAWBERRY
SOLSTICE CAKE

MAKES ONE 6-INCH THREE-LAYER CAKE

Summer solstice is the longest day of the year and marks the start of summer. My family loves to celebrate this event by coming together outdoors, wearing flower crowns, and making lots of delicious food. This recipe is a chiffon cake, which is lighter than a regular cake, and is also layered with whipped cream. Combined, these two things provide the perfect backdrop for the fresh lemon and strawberries.

THE THINGS YOU'LL NEED

Lemon Chiffon Cake
1 cup cake flour
½ cup plus 2 tablespoons sugar
1¼ teaspoons baking powder
¼ teaspoon salt
¼ cup vegetable oil
3 large eggs, separated
1½ teaspoons grated lemon zest
2 tablespoons lemon juice
2 tablespoons water
1 teaspoon vanilla extract

Decorations
1 batch Whipped Cream (page 20)
2 cups sliced strawberries
Small whole strawberries

LET'S GET STARTED!

1. Preheat the oven to 350°F. Line the bottoms of three 6-inch round cake pans with parchment paper.
2. Make the lemon chiffon cake: In a large bowl, sift together the cake flour, ½ cup of the sugar, the baking powder, and the salt. Whisk together and make a well in the center.
3. In a medium bowl, with an electric mixer, beat together the oil, egg yolks, lemon zest, lemon juice, and water until smooth and light.
4. Pour the egg yolk mixture into the flour mixture and whisk just until no dry streaks remain.
5. In a large bowl, with an electric mixer, beat the egg whites and vanilla until frothy, about 4 minutes. Continue beating, slowly adding the remaining 2 tablespoons sugar, until stiff peaks form.
6. Using a spatula, fold one-third of the egg whites into the batter and mix until well combined. Repeat this process two more times.
7. Divide the batter evenly among the prepared pans. Bake until the cake is golden brown and springs back when lightly touched, 30 to 35 minutes.
8. Let cool in the pans for 15 minutes, then turn out onto a wire rack to cool completely.
9. Level off the tops with a cake leveler or a large serrated knife.

TIME TO DECORATE!

1. Make the Whipped Cream.
2. Stack the cakes with whipped cream and sliced strawberries in between the layers.
3. Top with whipped cream and whole strawberries.

My sister and me rockin' summer flower crowns

ICE CREAM CONE CUPCAKES

MAKES 12 CUPCAKES

Cupcakes that look like ice cream cones? Count me in! This is a super simple recipe that is also cute and creative. Just fill a waffle cone halfway with cake batter and bake, then frost to look like a scoop of ice cream. These cupcakes may not cool you off, but they are the perfect summer treat.

THE THINGS YOU'LL NEED

Coconut Cake
3 tablespoons unsalted butter, melted
½ cup granulated sugar
1 large egg
½ teaspoon almond extract
¼ cup coconut milk
¾ cup self-rising flour
½ cup sweetened shredded coconut

Decorations
12 waffle ice cream cones (Keebler)
2 batches Vegan Buttercream Frosting (page 17)
2 cups powdered sugar
¾ cup dark chocolate coating wafers (Ghirardelli)
Rainbow nonpareils
12 maraschino cherries

Equipment
Cone baking rack
#824 decorating tip

LET'S GET STARTED!

1. Preheat the oven to 350°F. Place the cone baking rack on a baking sheet and fill each slot with an ice cream cone.
2. In a large bowl, whisk together the melted butter, granulated sugar, egg, almond extract, and coconut milk.
3. Add the flour and shredded coconut and mix until well combined.
4. Fill the cones halfway with the batter.
5. Bake until a wooden pick inserted into the center of a cupcake comes out clean, 18 to 20 minutes.
6. Let cool in the rack.

TIME TO DECORATE!

1. Make the Vegan Buttercream Frosting. Scoop 1 cup of frosting into a decorating bag fitted with a #824 tip.
2. Mix the powdered sugar into the remaining frosting until smooth. Using an ice cream scoop, scoop about 3 tablespoons of frosting onto each cupcake to look like ice cream.
3. Melt the chocolate and drizzle 1 tablespoon onto each cupcake, letting it drip down to look like hot fudge. Allow to set.
4. Pipe frosting onto each cupcake to look like a whipped cream swirl.
5. Sprinkle rainbow nonpareils onto each frosting swirl and top with a maraschino cherry.

HAVE A SWEET
SUMMER!

CHOCOLATE FUDGE STARS

MAKES 2 DOZEN STARS

Ah, fudge! If you've never had homemade chocolate fudge, now is the time to start. I'm always in the mood for chocolate, and if I want something smooth and creamy, there's no better choice. I make them bite-size to share with others.

THE THINGS YOU'LL NEED

Fudge
5 ounces milk chocolate, chopped
3 cups mini marshmallows (Jet-Puffed)
1 teaspoon vanilla extract
1½ cups sugar
8 tablespoons (1 stick) unsalted butter
Pinch of salt
½ cup heavy cream

Decorations
Nonpareils: red, white, and blue

Equipment
Small silicone star mold (1½-inch-wide x ¾-inch-deep cavities)
Stand mixer fitted with the paddle attachment
Small heavy-bottomed saucepan (do not use a nonstick pan)
Candy thermometer

LET'S GET STARTED!

1. Grease a silicone star mold with cooking spray.
2. Place the milk chocolate, marshmallows, and vanilla in the bowl of a stand mixer fitted with the paddle attachment.
3. In a small heavy-bottomed saucepan fitted with a candy thermometer, combine the sugar, butter, salt, and heavy cream. Bring the mixture to 240°F over medium heat, stirring every few minutes with a heat-resistant spatula.
4. With the mixer on low speed, slowly pour the hot sugar mixture into the bowl and beat until fully combined and smooth.
5. Carefully spoon the fudge into the greased silicone mold cavities.

TIME TO DECORATE!

1. Sprinkle nonpareils onto the top of each star and press lightly.
2. Refrigerate until set, about 1 hour.

MIXED BERRY JAR CAKE

—————————— MAKES 12 JAR CAKES ——————————

When I tried angel food cake for the first time I asked my mom if I was eating a cloud. This made her laugh because it's a type of cake that's light as air and tastes divine. These are perfect for any picnic or outdoor party. A fluffy, sweet snack in a jar. Yummy!

THE THINGS YOU'LL NEED

Angel Food Cake
1 cup cake flour
½ cup plus 1 cup sugar
9 large egg whites
1 teaspoon vanilla extract
1 teaspoon cream of tartar
¼ teaspoon salt

Decorations
2 batches Whipped Cream (page 20)
3 cups blueberries
15 large strawberries, cut into ¼-inch chunks
1½ cups raspberries
12 small strawberries

Equipment
12 wide-mouth ½-pint mason jars
Round cookie cutter (same size as opening of jar)

LET'S GET STARTED!

1. Preheat the oven to 350°F. Line a 9 x 13-inch baking pan with parchment paper.
2. Make the angel food cake: In a small bowl, sift together the flour and ½ cup of the sugar.
3. In a large bowl, with an electric mixer, whip the egg whites, vanilla, cream of tartar, and salt until soft peaks form. Slowly add the remaining 1 cup sugar and whip until stiff peaks form.
4. Fold one-third of the flour mixture into the egg white mixture. Gently fold in the remaining flour mixture just until no white streaks remain (do not overmix).
5. Pour the batter into the prepared pan and bake until a wooden pick inserted into the center comes out clean, 15 to 18 minutes.
6. Let cool in the pan on a wire rack until it reaches room temperature. Freeze for 30 minutes.

TIME TO DECORATE!

1. Make the Whipped Cream. Scoop into a decorating bag and cut the tip.
2. Using the round cookie cutter, cut out small rounds from the chilled cake.
3. Reserve some blueberries and raspberries for the topping. Fill the mason jars in layers: blueberries, whipped cream, a cake round, whipped cream, chopped strawberries, raspberries, whipped cream, a cake round.
4. Top with whipped cream, the reserved blueberries and raspberries, and the small strawberries.

HALLOWEEN

CANDY BAR WITCH FINGERS

MAKES 2 DOZEN FINGERS

Halloween is my absolute favorite holiday. There's pumpkins, candy, costumes, spooky decorations, fun parties, watching Hocus Pocus, *and adorable trick-or-treaters. Growing up, I loved dressing like a witch and trick-or-treating with my family. The one candy I always looked forward to getting the most was Butterfingers. This recipe is inspired by the beloved candy and brings the term "finger food" to a whole new level. Hope you enjoy this chocolate-covered flaky, peanut butter candy bar as much as I do.*

THE THINGS YOU'LL NEED

Honey Peanut Butter Candy
2 tablespoons water
¼ cup honey
½ cup maple syrup
¾ cup creamy peanut butter
2 teaspoons vanilla extract
2 teaspoons salt
4 cups chocolate coating wafers
    (Ghirardelli)

Decorations
1 batch Royal Icing (page 16)
Green food coloring

Equipment
Medium heavy-bottomed saucepan
    (do not use a nonstick pan)
Candy thermometer
Witch finger pan (Wilton)

LET'S GET STARTED!

1. Line the bottom of a 9 x 13-inch rimmed baking sheet with parchment paper and grease the paper and sides of the pan.
2. In a medium heavy-bottomed saucepan fitted with a candy thermometer, mix the water, honey, and maple syrup.
3. Bring the mixture to 300°F over medium heat without stirring it. Remove from the heat and quickly mix in the peanut butter, vanilla, and salt until well combined.
4. Pour the candy mixture into the prepared pan and spread to ¼ inch thick. Let cool for 15 minutes.
5. Use a sharp knife to mark 2¾ x ½-inch rectangles onto the warm candy. Let cool for 1 hour.

Me as a spooky witch

My sister as Wednesday from The Addams Family

• CONTINUES •

6. Remove the candy from the pan and cut along the marked lines to create rectangles (A).
7. Melt the chocolate and brush a thin layer in each cavity of the witch finger mold (B). Let set for 5 minutes.
8. Scoop the remaining chocolate into a decorating bag and cut the tip. Pipe the chocolate into the cavities, filling them about one-quarter full, and gently press in the candy rectangles (C). Save the remaining chocolate for more batches and reheat as needed.
9. Fill the rest of the cavity with chocolate. Tap the mold on the counter to release any air bubbles. Freeze for 20 minutes.
10. Pop the candies out by turning the mold upside down and tapping it against a hard surface.

TIME TO DECORATE!

1. Make the Royal Icing. Tint green and paint each fingernail (D).

CANDY CORN COOKIES

MAKES 15 COOKIES

Candy corn in a cookie? It's actually better than it sounds. While opinions on this traditional Halloween candy vary, the one thing everyone will agree on is how yummy these cookies are. They are similar to soft white chocolate macadamia nut cookies, but instead of nuts there's candy!

THE THINGS YOU'LL NEED

18 large marshmallows (Jet-Puffed)
2 teaspoons water
1½ cups all-purpose flour
½ teaspoon baking soda
⅛ teaspoon baking powder
½ teaspoon salt
8 tablespoons (1 stick) unsalted butter, cold
¼ cup granulated sugar
¼ cup packed light brown sugar
1 large egg
½ teaspoon vanilla extract
⅓ cup white chocolate chips (Nestlé)
⅓ cup coarsely chopped candy corn
½ cup whole candy corn

LET'S GET STARTED!

1. Preheat the oven to 350°F. Line 2 baking sheets with parchment paper.
2. Melt the marshmallows and water to make a smooth marshmallow crème.
3. In a medium bowl, whisk together the flour, baking soda, baking powder, and salt.
4. In a large bowl, with an electric mixer, beat the butter, granulated sugar, brown sugar, and marshmallow crème until light and fluffy, 3 to 5 minutes.
5. Beat in the egg and vanilla.
6. On low speed, beat in the flour mixture until combined.
7. Using a spatula, fold in the white chocolate chips and chopped candy corn.
8. Place 2-tablespoon scoops of the dough 2 inches apart on the baking sheets.
9. Bake for 8 minutes. Remove the pans from the oven and carefully place a few whole candy corns on top of each cookie. Bake until the edges are golden brown, about 3 minutes longer.
10. Let cool on the baking sheets for 2 minutes, then transfer to a wire rack to cool completely.

BAT TRUFFLES

How cute are these bats? When I first saw bats in Halloween vampire movies, I thought they were scary looking. It wasn't until a little later that my parents took my sister and me to the Carlsbad Bat Caverns in New Mexico that I learned more about this amazing animal. I created this recipe to pay homage to our often misunderstood winged friends. This recipe has caramel, chocolate, and peanut butter, which is fangtastic if you ask me.

THE THINGS YOU'LL NEED

Caramel Chocolate Peanut Butter Truffles
½ cup granulated sugar
½ cup packed light brown sugar
1 tablespoon corn syrup
3 tablespoons water
½ cup heavy cream
Pinch of salt
¼ teaspoon almond extract
½ teaspoon vanilla extract
6 ounces dark chocolate, chopped
¼ cup creamy peanut butter

Decorations
2 cups dark chocolate coating
    wafers (Ghirardelli)
Chocolate-coated sunflower seeds
Bat wings template (page 249)
Small candy eyeballs (Wilton)
1 batch Royal Icing (page 16)

Equipment
Medium heavy-bottomed saucepan
    (do not use a nonstick pan)
Candy thermometer
Two #1 decorating tips

LET'S GET STARTED!

1. In a medium heavy-bottomed saucepan fitted with a candy thermometer, mix together the granulated sugar, brown sugar, corn syrup, and water. Bring to 275°F over medium-high heat, stirring constantly.
2. Add the heavy cream and stir until smooth and well combined.
3. Remove the saucepan from the heat and whisk in the salt, almond extract, and vanilla.
4. Keep whisking until the mixture cools to 150°F, then whisk in the chopped chocolate until smooth.
5. Whisk in the peanut butter.
6. Pour the mixture into a clean bowl and refrigerate until firm, about 1 hour.
7. Line a baking sheet with parchment paper. Roll 1 tablespoon of chilled chocolate mixture into a ball and place it on the baking sheet. Repeat until all of the truffle mixture is used.
8. Refrigerate the truffle balls for 15 minutes.

• CONTINUES •

1. Melt the chocolate. Place the truffles in the chocolate and completely cover using a fork. Place the dipped truffles on wax paper. While the chocolate is still wet, position 2 chocolate-coated sunflower seeds for ears **A**.

2. Place the bat wings template on a clean baking sheet and cover with a piece of wax paper.

3. Scoop the remaining coating chocolate into a decorating bag fitted with a #1 tip. Outline each wing, then fill in **B**. Set aside to dry completely.

4. Peel the wings from the wax paper and attach to the back of the truffle with melted chocolate **C**.

5. Attach 2 candy eyeballs to each bat with melted chocolate.

6. Make the Royal Icing and scoop it into a decorating bag fitted with a #1 tip.

7. Pipe white mouths and fangs **D**.

BREADSTICK BONES

There's nothing better than a basket of warm breadsticks on a chilly evening. Especially when they are potato breadsticks with a hint of garlic, shaped like bones, and topped with cheese. An added bonus is that the garlic will keep vampires away. Dip these in marinara sauce for an extra creepy garnish. You can bake some ahead of time and reheat them later. Bone appétit!

THE THINGS YOU'LL NEED

Dough
1¼ teaspoons active dry yeast
¼ cup warm whole milk
¼ cup warm water
2 tablespoons sugar
¼ cup mashed potatoes
4 tablespoons unsalted butter, melted
1 large egg
1 cup all-purpose flour
1¼ cups bread flour
½ teaspoon garlic powder
2 teaspoons salt
1 tablespoon olive oil, for coating the bowl and dough

Topping
4 tablespoons unsalted butter, melted
1 teaspoon garlic powder
½ cup grated Asiago cheese

Equipment
Stand mixer fitted with the dough hook

LET'S GET STARTED!

1. Make the dough: In the bowl of a stand mixer, whisk together the yeast, milk, water, and sugar. Set aside until foamy, about 10 minutes.
2. Once foamy, stir in the mashed potatoes, melted butter, and egg.
3. In a medium bowl, whisk together the all-purpose flour, bread flour, and garlic powder.
4. Stir ½ cup of the flour mixture into the yeast mixture until a thick paste forms.
5. With the mixer on low speed, beat in the salt and the remaining flour mixture, ¼ cup at a time. Mix until the dough is soft and pulls away from the sides of the bowl, 3 to 5 minutes.
6. On a lightly floured surface, knead the dough for an additional minute, then form into a large ball. If the dough is too sticky, add more flour as needed.
7. Grease a large bowl with the olive oil and place the dough inside. Roll the dough in the oil to completely coat. Cover the bowl with a clean cloth and let rest at room temperature until doubled in size, 1 to 2 hours.
8. Preheat the oven to 350°F. Line 2 baking sheets with parchment paper and lightly grease the paper.
9. On a lightly floured surface, divide the dough into 18 portions and shape each portion into a ball. Keep the dough covered with a clean cloth to prevent a skin from forming.

• CONTINUES •

10. Roll the balls into 4-inch ropes with a bulge at each end **A**. Place on the baking sheets.
11. Cut the ends of the breadsticks to create bone details **B**.
12. Cover the breadsticks with a clean cloth and let rest for 15 minutes.
13. Bake the bones until golden brown, 12 to 14 minutes.
14. Make the topping: In a small bowl, stir together the melted butter and garlic powder.
15. Brush the garlic butter onto the warm breadsticks **C** and sprinkle with the Asiago **D**.

MONSTER
CRISPY TREATS

Let's be frank, I can't help but watch lots of spooky monster movies during the month of October. This recipe is inspired by one of the most iconic monsters and isn't a pain in the neck to make. They're mint chocolate chip flavored and they're frightfully fantastic.

THE THINGS YOU'LL NEED

Mint Chocolate Chip Crispy Treats
3 tablespoons salted butter
4½ cups mini marshmallows (Jet-Puffed)
¼ teaspoon peppermint extract
Green food coloring
6 cups puffed rice cereal (Rice Krispies)
1 cup mini chocolate chips (Nestlé)

Decorations
1 batch Royal Icing (page 16)
Green food coloring
1½ cups dark coating chocolate wafers (Ghirardelli)
Large candy eyeballs (Wilton)
12 mini marshmallows (Jet-Puffed)

Equipment
Decorating tips: #2, #3

LET'S GET STARTED!

1. Grease a 9 x 13-inch metal baking pan and line the bottom and two sides of the pan with parchment paper (leave an overhang to make it easier to take out of the pan).
2. In a large saucepan, melt the butter over low heat and add the marshmallows. Stir constantly until the marshmallows are melted, about 6 minutes. Remove from the heat.
3. Stir in the peppermint extract and green food coloring until well combined.
4. Add the cereal and stir until evenly coated. Fold in the mini chocolate chips, working quickly so the chocolate does not melt.
5. Press the mixture firmly into the bottom of the prepared pan.
6. Let cool completely, about 25 minutes.
7. Cut into 12 rectangles.

TIME TO DECORATE!

1. Make the Royal Icing. Tint green and scoop into a decorating bag fitted with a #3 tip. Outline the treats with the icing and let set.
2. Once the outline has hardened, fill in the center of the treats to make the face. Let dry completely, about 1 hour.
3. Melt the chocolate. Line a baking sheet with wax paper.
4. Dip 1 end of each treat into the melted chocolate for the hair and place on the baking sheet. Let dry.
5. Scoop the remaining melted chocolate into a decorating bag fitted with a #2 tip. Using the chocolate, attach candy eyeballs to each face. Pipe eyebrow and mouth details.
6. Cut the mini marshmallows in half crosswise. Using the green icing, attach a half on each side of the treat for the neck bolts.

◆ RO TIP ◆

To get the crispy mixture FLAT on the surface, place a piece of greased parchment paper over the top and smooth it out with your hand.

JACK-O'-LANTERN
COOKIE POPS

MAKES 2 DOZEN COOKIE POPS

It's a tradition in my family to go to a pumpkin patch and carve pumpkins every year. It just wouldn't be Halloween without some jack-o'-lanterns! I designed these spooktacular cookie pops to be gluten-free.

THE THINGS YOU'LL NEED

Chocolate Cookie

2 cups gluten-free 1-to-1 baking flour (Bob's Red Mill)

½ cup unsweetened dark cocoa powder (Hershey's Special Dark)

½ cup packed light brown sugar

¼ cup granulated sugar

¼ teaspoon salt

3 large eggs, at room temperature

8 tablespoons (1 stick) unsalted butter, melted and cooled

1½ teaspoons vanilla extract

Cream Filling

1 batch Vegan Buttercream Frosting (page 17)

2 cups powdered sugar, sifted

Seeds of ½ vanilla bean

Decorations

2 bags (12 ounces each) orange Candy Melts (Wilton)

1 bag (12 ounces) black Candy Melts (Wilton)

12 gluten-free pretzel sticks (Snyder's)

1 bag (12 ounces) green Candy Melts (Wilton)

Equipment

1¾-inch round cookie cutter (template on page 248)

24 lollipop sticks

Foam block

#1 decorating tip

LET'S GET STARTED!

1. Make the chocolate cookie: In a medium bowl, whisk together the gluten-free flour, cocoa powder, brown sugar, granulated sugar, and salt.

2. In a small bowl, whisk the eggs.

3. Make a well in the center of the flour mixture and add the beaten eggs, melted butter, and vanilla. Stir until well combined.

4. Shape the dough into a disk and wrap in plastic wrap. Refrigerate for at least 1 hour.

5. Preheat the oven to 325°F. Line 2 baking sheets with parchment paper.

6. On a lightly gluten-free floured surface, roll out the dough to ¼ inch thick. Cut out 48 cookies using the round cookie cutter and place them 1 inch apart on the baking sheets.

7. Bake until the cookies are firm to the touch, 8 to 10 minutes.

8. Let cool on the baking sheets for 2 minutes, then transfer to a wire rack to cool completely.

9. Make the cream filling: Make the Vegan Buttercream Frosting.

10. In a large bowl, with an electric mixer, beat the buttercream, powdered sugar, and vanilla seeds until smooth. Scoop the frosting into a decorating bag and cut the end.

11. Pipe a small mound of filling into the center of half the cookies. Place a lollipop stick into the center of the filling.

12. Top with an unfrosted cookie and gently press down to secure.

TIME TO DECORATE!

1. Melt the orange Candy Melts. Dip the cookies into the melted candy to cover completely. Stand the dipped cookies in a foam block to dry.

2. Melt the black Candy Melts and scoop into a decorating bag fitted with a #1 tip. Pipe on jack-o'-lantern faces.

3. Cut about ½ inch off each end of the 12 pretzel sticks (a total of 24 end pieces).

4. Melt the green Candy Melts. Dip the cut end of the pretzel into the green candy and attach to the top of the cookie for the pumpkin's stem.

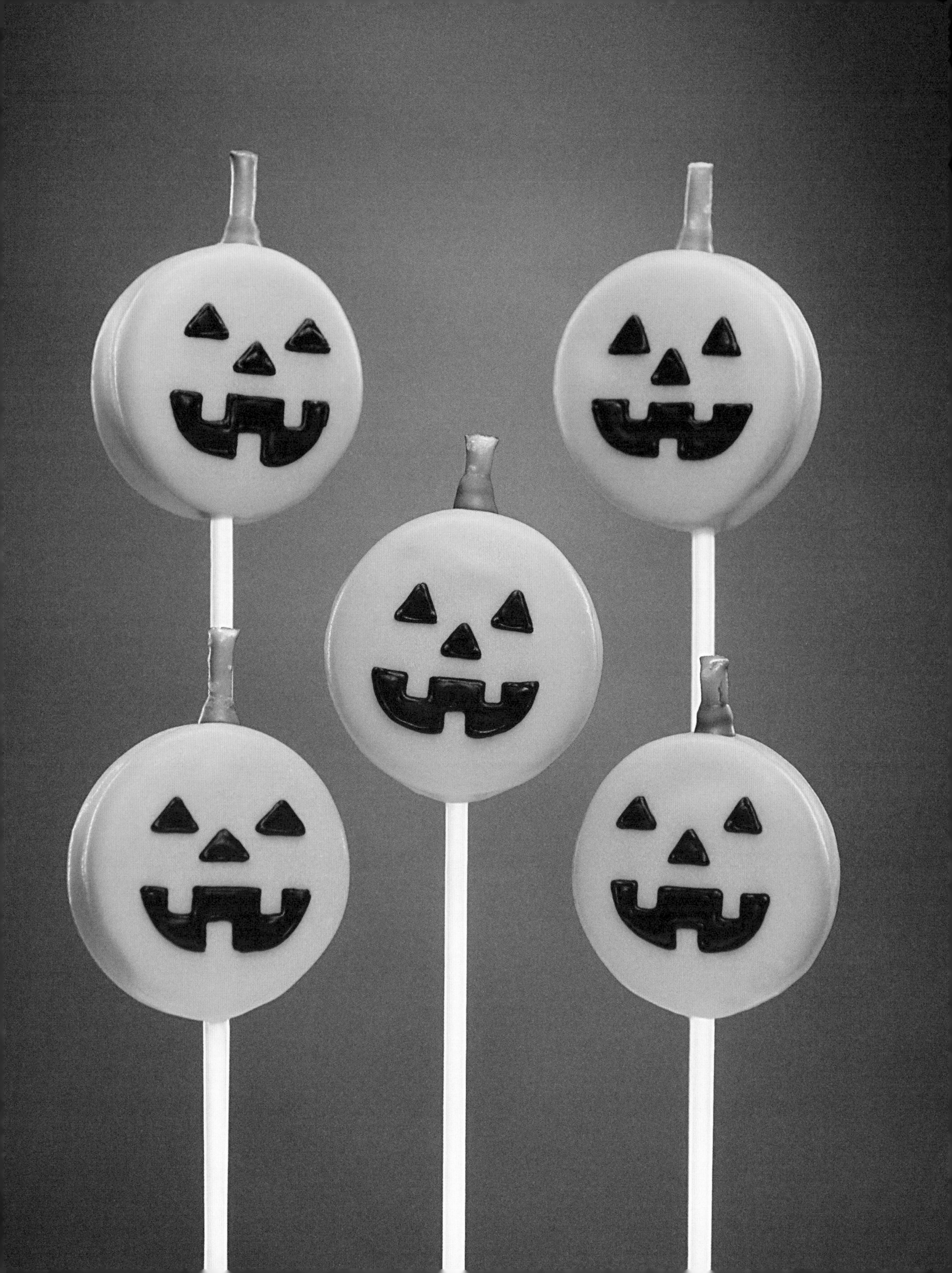

CARAMEL APPLE
MUMMY COOKIES

MAKES 16 COOKIES

Anyone else love caramel apples in the fall? I sure do, even though they are a little tricky to eat. Fear not, these mummies have all the taste of a caramel apple wrapped up in a delightful cookie.

THE THINGS YOU'LL NEED

Brown Butter Cookie Dough
4 sticks (16 ounces) unsalted butter
5 cups all-purpose flour
1 teaspoon baking powder
1 teaspoon salt
1 cup granulated sugar
1 cup packed dark brown sugar
4 large eggs
4 teaspoons vanilla extract

Caramel Apple Filling
2 tablespoons unsalted butter
4 large Granny Smith apples,
   peeled, cored, and cut into
   ¼-inch dice
10 soft caramels (Kraft)

Decoration
Small candy eyeballs (Wilton)

Equipment
Stand mixer fitted with the paddle
   attachment
5 x 2½-inch rectangle cookie cutter
   (template on page 249)

LET'S GET STARTED!

1. Make the brown butter cookie dough: In a small saucepan, melt the butter over medium heat, reduce the heat to low, and allow to brown, 12 to 15 minutes.
2. Pour into a heatproof bowl and freeze until firm, about 1 hour. Allow the butter to come back to room temperature before using.
3. In a medium bowl, whisk together the flour, baking powder, and salt.
4. In a stand mixer fitted with the paddle attachment, beat the brown butter, and sugars until light and fluffy, 3 to 5 minutes.
5. Add the eggs one at a time, beating well after each addition.
6. Beat in the vanilla.
7. On low speed, slowly add the flour mixture and beat until combined.
8. Shape the dough into a disk and wrap with plastic wrap. Refrigerate for at least 1 hour.
9. Make the caramel apple filling: In a nonstick skillet, melt the butter over medium heat. Add the apples and cook until soft, about 5 minutes. Add the caramels and cook until melted, about 2 minutes. Drain off excess liquid and let cool.
10. Line 2 baking sheets with parchment paper.
11. On a lightly floured surface, roll out the dough to a ¼-inch thickness. Cut out 16 cookies using the rectangle cutter. Cut out strips of dough 3 inches long and ¼ inch wide. (Each cookie uses about 9 strips.)
12. Place the rectangles 2 inches apart on the baking sheets. Spread about 2 teaspoons of filling evenly on each rectangle, leaving a small border. Place the dough strips over the filling to look like a wrapped mummy.
13. Freeze the cookies for 30 minutes.
14. Meanwhile, preheat the oven to 350°F.
15. Bake until the cookies are firm to the touch and lightly browned around the edges, about 20 minutes.
16. Let cool on the baking sheets for 10 minutes, then transfer to a wire rack to cool completely.

TIME TO DECORATE!

1. Place the candy eyeballs on the upper third of the cookies.

BRAIN CUPCAKES

MAKES 12 CUPCAKES

Braaaainnnnns! While I wouldn't recommend eating actual brains, I certainly won't try to stop you from eating cupcake brains. They may look gruesome but you won't regret whipping up these raspberry-flavored Brain Cupcakes.

THE THINGS YOU'LL NEED

Raspberry Cake

1¾ cups unsweetened frozen raspberries
¼ cup whole milk
¾ cup all-purpose flour
¾ cup cake flour
½ teaspoon baking powder
½ teaspoon baking soda
½ teaspoon salt
12 tablespoons (1½ sticks) unsalted butter, at room temperature
¾ cup sugar
2 large eggs
½ teaspoon vanilla extract
Red food coloring

Raspberry Blood Topping

½ cup seedless raspberry jam
1 tablespoon lemon juice
2 tablespoons water
Red food coloring

Decoration

1 batch Swiss Buttercream Frosting (page 17)

Equipment

Decorating tips: #1A, #10

LET'S GET STARTED!

1. Preheat the oven to 350°F. Line 12 cups of a muffin tin with liners.
2. Make the raspberry cake: In a microwave-safe bowl, microwave the raspberries until thawed, 60 to 90 seconds. In a blender puree the raspberries until smooth.
3. Strain the raspberry puree into a small bowl to remove the seeds. Whisk in the milk.
4. In a medium bowl, whisk together the all-purpose flour, cake flour, baking powder, baking soda, and salt.
5. In a large bowl, with an electric mixer, beat the butter and sugar until light and fluffy, 3 to 5 minutes.
6. Add the eggs one at a time, beating well after each addition.
7. Beat in the vanilla and 2 drops red food coloring.
8. With the mixer on low speed, alternate adding the flour mixture and the raspberry mixture to the butter mixture, beginning and ending with the flour mixture.
9. Fill each liner two-thirds full with batter and bake until a wooden pick inserted into the center of a cupcake comes out clean, 15 to 17 minutes.
10. Transfer to a wire rack to cool.

TIME TO DECORATE!

1. Make the raspberry blood topping: In a small saucepan, whisk together the jam, lemon juice, and water and bring to a boil over medium heat.
2. Remove from the heat and whisk in red food coloring. Let cool completely before use.
3. Make the Swiss Buttercream Frosting. Scoop half the frosting into a decorating bag fitted with a #1A tip and pipe a small mound of frosting on top of each cupcake.
4. Scoop the remaining frosting into a decorating bag fitted with a #10 tip and pipe a brain design on each mound.
5. Drizzle with the raspberry blood.

CHAPTER SEVEN

THANKSGIVING

MINI PUMPKIN CAKES

MAKES 12 MINI PUMPKINS

From the moment I tried my first pumpkin spice latte I was hooked. It was love at first sip. These little cakes are made with my Pumpkin Spice Latte Cake recipe to taste just like the drink. They are also decorated with Swiss Buttercream Espresso Frosting. Swiss buttercream is exceptionally smooth and soft and well worth the time to make. If you like PSLs as much as I do (my boyfriend's nickname for me is "Pumpkin Spice") then this is the recipe for you.

THE THINGS YOU'LL NEED

Pumpkin Spice Latte Cake

1⅔ cups all-purpose flour
1½ teaspoons baking powder
1½ teaspoons pumpkin pie spice
½ teaspoon salt
8 tablespoons (1 stick) unsalted butter, melted
2 tablespoons espresso powder
½ cup granulated sugar
⅔ cup packed light brown sugar
1 cup canned unsweetened pumpkin puree
2 large eggs

Decorations

2 batches Swiss Buttercream Frosting (page 17)
½ cup brewed espresso
Food coloring: orange and green
12 chocolate candy rolls (Tootsie Roll)

Equipment

Two 12-cavity mini fluted pans (Wilton)
Decorating tips: #2, #352

LET'S GET STARTED!

1. Preheat the oven to 350°F. Lightly grease two 12-cavity mini fluted pans.
2. In a medium bowl, whisk together the flour, baking powder, pumpkin pie spice, and salt.
3. In a large bowl, mix together the melted butter and espresso powder. Whisk in the granulated sugar, brown sugar, pumpkin puree, and eggs until smooth.
4. Add the flour mixture to the wet ingredients and mix just until no dry streaks remain (do not overmix).
5. Fill each pan cavity halfway with batter. Bake until a wooden pick inserted halfway between the edge and the center comes out clean, 10 to 12 minutes.
6. Let cool in the pans for 15 minutes, then transfer the cakes to a wire rack to cool completely.

TIME TO DECORATE!

1. Make the Swiss Buttercream Frosting. While the frosting is still in the mixer bowl, beat in the brewed espresso until well combined.
2. Divide the frosting between 2 bowls, three-quarters in one bowl and one-quarter in the second bowl. Tint the larger amount of buttercream orange and tint the smaller green. Scoop the green frosting into separate decorating bags, one fitted with a #2 tip and the other with a #352 tip.

• CONTINUES •

3. Level off the tops of the cakes with a cake leveler or a small serrated knife Ⓐ.
4. Stack the cakes, leveled sides together, spreading a thin layer of orange frosting in between, to form pumpkins Ⓑ.
5. Frost the entire cake with orange buttercream. Gently run the tip of a small offset spatula from the bottom to the top to create the texture of the pumpkin Ⓒ.
6. Shape each Tootsie Roll into a stem. Place one in the center of each pumpkin.
7. Using the #2 tip, pipe vines around the stem. Using the #352 tip, pipe leaves onto the vines Ⓓ.

PEAR CRUMBLE
CORNUCOPIAS

MAKES 18 TO 22 PASTRIES

Overflowing with sweetened pear and a cinnamon crumble, these edible cornucopias make the pearfect after-dinner treat. I always find a warm crumble comforting in fall when the air begins to turn crisper. The last few years, I've hosted family at my house for dinner, which means lots of wholesome dishes for everyone to try.

THE THINGS YOU'LL NEED

Pastry Horns

1 box (17.3 ounces) frozen puff
   pastry (Pepperidge Farm),
   thawed
Egg wash: 1 large egg beaten with a
   pinch of salt

Crumble Topping

1 cup packed light brown sugar
¾ cup all-purpose flour
¾ cup old-fashioned rolled oats
1 teaspoon ground cinnamon
¼ teaspoon salt
8 tablespoons (1 stick) unsalted
   butter, cut into cubes and chilled

Pear Filling

4 tablespoons unsalted butter
6 medium pears, peeled, cored, and
   cut into ½-inch dice
¼ cup granulated sugar

Equipment

12 metal cream horn molds
   (4¼ x 1½ inches)

LET'S GET STARTED!

1. Preheat the oven to 400°F. Line 2 baking sheets with parchment paper.
2. Make the pastry horns: Cut the puff pastry crosswise into strips ½ inch wide (A). Pinch two strips together and wrap around the metal mold, starting at the tip and working toward the wide end (B). Pinch the end of the strip to the dough to seal and place seam side down on the baking sheets. Repeat with the remaining molds to make 12 pastries. Cover and refrigerate the unused pastry strips.
3. Freeze the wrapped molds for 10 minutes.
4. Brush all the pastries with egg wash (C) and bake until golden brown, 18 to 20 minutes. (Leave the oven on.) Let the pastries cool to room temperature, then remove the molds (D). Repeat with the remaining pastry strips to bake more pastry horns.
5. Make the crumble topping: Reduce the oven temperature to 350°F. Line a baking sheet with parchment paper.
6. In a medium bowl, with an electric mixer, mix together the brown sugar, flour, oats, cinnamon, salt, and cold butter until the mixture has a crumbly texture.
7. Spread the mixture onto the prepared baking sheet and bake until golden brown, 8 to 12 minutes. When cool, break into small pieces.

• CONTINUES •

8. Make the pear filling: In a skillet, melt 1 tablespoon of the butter over medium heat. Add one-quarter of the pears and sprinkle with 1 tablespoon of the granulated sugar. Cook until soft, about 5 minutes. Transfer to a bowl. Continue cooking the pears in batches, using the remaining butter and sugar.

TIME TO DECORATE!

1. Fill each pastry horn with pear filling so that it is spilling out from the opening of the "cornucopia."
2. Sprinkle the crumble on top of the pear filling.

AUTUMN LEAF COOKIES

The changing color of leaves signifies that fall has finally arrived and it's officially time for sweater weather. I thought it would be fun to create a recipe that captures the beauty of autumn by combining colorful cookie dough, thus making each leaf cookie as unique and beautiful as the real thing. They are also gluten- and dairy-free, which will leaf your friends and family wanting more.

THE THINGS YOU'LL NEED

Vanilla Almond Sugar Cookies
2¼ cups gluten-free 1-to-1 baking flour (Bob's Red Mill)
¼ teaspoon baking soda
¼ teaspoon salt
10 tablespoons vegetable shortening
1 cup granulated sugar
1 large egg
1 teaspoon almond extract
½ teaspoon vanilla extract
Food coloring: red, orange, and yellow

Decoration
Coarse white sanding sugar

Equipment
Autumn leaf cookie cutter (template on page 250)

LET'S GET STARTED!

1. In a medium bowl, whisk together the flour, baking soda, and salt.
2. In a large bowl, with an electric mixer, beat the shortening and granulated sugar until light and fluffy, 3 to 5 minutes.
3. Add the egg and beat well.
4. Beat in the almond extract and vanilla.
5. On low speed, beat in the flour mixture until combined.
6. Divide the dough into 3 equal portions. Tint each portion with a different food coloring: red, orange, and yellow.
7. Shape each colored dough into a disk and wrap in plastic wrap. Refrigerate for at least 1 hour.
8. Preheat the oven to 350°F. Line 2 baking sheets with parchment paper.

In my first fall leaf pile

• CONTINUES •

1. On a lightly floured surface, tear the dough into 2-inch portions
   Ⓐ and patch together in alternating colors Ⓑ. Roll out the
   patched dough to create a marbled sheet.
2. Cut out cookies using the leaf cookie cutter Ⓒ and place them
   1 inch apart on the baking sheets. Sprinkle with sanding sugar Ⓓ.
3. Freeze the cookies for 10 minutes.
4. Bake until the cookies are firm to the touch but not browned on
   the edges, 10 to 12 minutes.
5. Let cool on the baking sheets for 2 minutes, then transfer to a
   wire rack to cool completely.

PUMPKIN PIE COOKIES

— MAKES 12 COOKIES —

Cookies that taste like pie? I think I've found one of my new favorite things. These cookies bring together the best parts of cookie dough and piecrust and are topped with a classic pumpkin pie filling.

THE THINGS YOU'LL NEED

Pie Dough
2 cups all-purpose flour
¼ cup granulated sugar
1 teaspoon salt
2 sticks (8 ounces) unsalted butter, cut into cubes and chilled
2 large egg yolks
¼ cup ice-cold water

Pumpkin Filling
1 cup canned unsweetened pumpkin puree
2 teaspoons packed light brown sugar
½ teaspoon pumpkin pie spice
¼ teaspoon salt
Egg wash: 1 large egg beaten with a pinch of salt

Decoration
1 batch Whipped Cream (page 20)

Equipment
Stand mixer fitted with the paddle attachment
Round cookie cutters: 2¼ inch and 1½ inch (templates on page 251)
#824 decorating tip

LET'S GET STARTED!

1. Make the pie dough: In a stand mixer fitted with the paddle attachment, mix together the flour, granulated sugar, salt, butter and egg yolks on low speed until a coarse meal forms. Add just enough cold water so that the dough holds together when pinched. Shape the dough into a disk and wrap in plastic wrap. Refrigerate for 3 to 4 hours.
2. Make the pumpkin filling: In a bowl, whisk together the pumpkin puree, brown sugar, pumpkin pie spice, and salt until well combined.
3. Preheat the oven to 400°F. Line a baking sheet with parchment paper.
4. On a lightly floured surface, roll out the dough to a ¼-inch thickness. Cut out 24 cookies using the 2¼-inch round cookie cutter.
5. Cut out centers from half the cookies using the 1½-inch round cookie cutter.
6. Brush egg wash on the edges of the whole cookies and place the cut cookies on top.
7. Scoop 2 teaspoons of filling into the center of each cookie.
8. Freeze for 10 minutes.
9. Bake until the cookies are lightly browned around the edges, 15 to 18 minutes.
10. Let cool on the baking sheet.

TIME TO DECORATE!

1. Make the Whipped Cream.
2. Scoop the whipped cream into a decorating bag fitted with a #824 tip and pipe a small swirl in the center of each cookie.

MAPLE PECAN BLONDIES

MAKES 3 DOZEN BLONDIES

If you've ever wondered what fall tastes like then look no further. Maple Pecan Blondies are like if a pecan pie and a maple bar donut had a baby. Incredible.

THE THINGS YOU'LL NEED

Pecan Blondies

2 cups gluten-free 1-to-1 baking flour (Bob's Red Mill)
1 teaspoon baking powder
1 teaspoon ground cinnamon
¼ teaspoon baking soda
¼ teaspoon salt
⅔ cup unsalted butter
2 cups packed light brown sugar
2 large eggs
1 teaspoon vanilla extract
1 cup ground pecans
1½ to 2 cups pecan halves

Maple Glaze

2 tablespoons maple syrup
1 cup powdered sugar, sifted

LET'S GET STARTED!

1. Preheat the oven to 325°F. Grease a 9 x 13-inch metal baking pan and line the bottom and sides of the pan with parchment paper.
2. Make the pecan blondies: In a large bowl, whisk together the flour, baking powder, cinnamon, baking soda, and salt.
3. In a small saucepan, melt the butter and brown sugar over medium heat. Remove from the heat and let cool for 10 minutes at room temperature.
4. Whisk the eggs and vanilla into the butter mixture.
5. Make a well in the center of the flour mixture and add the butter mixture. Stir just until no dry streaks of flour remain (do not overmix).
6. Fold in the ground pecans.
7. Scoop the batter into the prepared pan and spread evenly. Cover the top with the pecans.
8. Bake until a wooden pick inserted into the center comes out clean, 20 to 22 minutes.
9. Let cool in the pan on a wire rack until it reaches room temperature.
10. Make the maple glaze: In a bowl, whisk together the maple syrup and powdered sugar until smooth.
11. Cut the blondies into 36 squares and drizzle with the glaze.

ACORN CAKE POPS

These Acorn Cake Pops are fun to bring to parties because they transport easily and don't make a mess. Maybe the local squirrels were on to something. Go nuts!

THE THINGS YOU'LL NEED

Walnut Cake Balls

¾ cup plus 2 tablespoons all-purpose flour
½ teaspoon baking soda
Pinch of salt
6 tablespoons ground walnuts
2 tablespoons unsalted butter, at room temperature
2 tablespoons vegetable shortening
½ cup sugar
1 large egg
½ teaspoon vanilla extract
6 tablespoons buttermilk
¼ cup Dark Chocolate Frosting (page 19)

Decorations

4 cups dark chocolate coating wafers (Ghirardelli)
½ cup ground walnuts
12 pretzel sticks (Snyder's)

Equipment

Stand mixer fitted with the paddle attachment
24 lollipop sticks
Foam block

LET'S GET STARTED!

1. Preheat the oven to 350°F. Grease an 8-inch round cake pan and line the bottom with a round of parchment paper.
2. In a medium bowl, whisk together the flour, baking soda, salt, and ground walnuts.
3. In a stand mixer fitted with the paddle attachment, beat the butter, shortening, and sugar until light and fluffy, 3 to 5 minutes.
4. Add the egg and beat well.
5. Beat in the vanilla.
6. On low speed, alternate adding the flour mixture and the buttermilk to the butter mixture, beginning and ending with the flour mixture.
7. Pour the batter into the prepared pan and bake until a wooden pick inserted into the center comes out clean, 20 to 23 minutes.
8. Let cool in the pan on a wire rack until it reaches room temperature.
9. Break the cake into pieces into the bowl of a stand mixer fitted with the paddle attachment. Add the frosting. On low speed, beat until a dough-like mixture forms, 3 to 5 minutes.
10. Line a baking sheet with wax paper. Roll 1 tablespoon of cake dough into an acorn shape and place on the lined baking sheet. Repeat to make 24 cake balls.
11. Refrigerate the cake balls until set, about 30 minutes.

TIME TO DECORATE!

1. Melt the chocolate. Dip one end of a lollipop stick into the chocolate, then insert it halfway into an acorn at an angle.
2. Dip the acorn balls into the chocolate and cover completely. Stand the dipped acorns in a foam block to dry. Let the chocolate dry completely, about 15 minutes.
3. Dip the top of each acorn ball in the melted chocolate and cover with ground walnuts for the acorn cap.
4. Cover the pretzel sticks in chocolate and let dry. Cut about ½ inch off each end of a pretzel. Dip the cut end into chocolate and attach at the top of the acorn for the stem.

HARVEST CORN COOKIES

One of the best things about fall is the harvest festivals. My family eagerly awaits their arrival to experience the corn mazes, chili cook-offs, hayrides, and pumpkin patches. We always return with ears of colorful corn to decorate our house. These peanut butter cookies with a honey buttercream frosting look like the real thing and are surprisingly easy to decorate.

THE THINGS YOU'LL NEED

Peanut Butter Cookies

4 cups all-purpose flour
2 tablespoons cornstarch
1½ teaspoons salt
2 sticks (8 ounces) unsalted butter, at room temperature
1 cup creamy peanut butter
1 cup granulated sugar
1 cup packed light brown sugar
2 large eggs
1 teaspoon vanilla extract

Decorations

1 batch Honey Buttercream Frosting (page 19)
1½ teaspoons gold food coloring (AmeriColor)
Candy-coated peanut butter pieces (Reese's Pieces)

Equipment

Corncob cookie cutter (template on page 248)
Maple leaf cookie cutter (template on page 250)
Decorating tips: #10, #366

LET'S GET STARTED!

1. In a medium bowl, whisk together the flour, cornstarch, and salt.
2. In a large bowl, with an electric mixer, beat the butter, peanut butter, granulated sugar, and brown sugar until light and fluffy, 3 to 5 minutes.
3. Add the eggs one at a time, beating well after each addition.
4. Beat in the vanilla.
5. On low speed, beat in the flour mixture until combined.
6. Shape the dough into a disk and wrap in plastic wrap. Refrigerate for at least 1 hour.
7. Preheat the oven to 350°F. Line 3 baking sheets with parchment paper.
8. On a sheet of parchment, roll out the dough to a ¼-inch thickness. Cut out equal numbers of corncob and maple leaf cookies with the cookie cutters.

• CONTINUES •

9. Cut the bottoms of the maple leaf cookies with the bottom of the corncob cookie cutter (A).

10. Place a corncob cookie into the cut area of a maple leaf cookie and press the seams together (B). Place the cookies 2 inches apart on the baking sheets.

11. Freeze the cookies for 15 minutes.

12. Bake until firm to the touch but not browned at the edges, 10 to 12 minutes.

13. Let cool on the baking sheets for 2 minutes, then transfer to a wire rack to cool completely.

TIME TO DECORATE!

1. Make the Honey Buttercream Frosting. Tint gold and scoop into separate decorating bags fitted with #10 and #366 tips. Reserve the remaining frosting for refilling the decorating bags as needed.

2. Outline the corncob of the cookie using the #10 tip, then fill in the center. Arrange the candies on top of the frosting to look like corn kernels (C).

3. Using the #366 tip, pipe a cornhusk leaf design on the remaining part of the cookie (D). Refill the decorating bag as needed.

PUMPKIN DINNER ROLLS

Warm, golden, and soft are the three words I would use to describe the perfect dinner roll. If you're someone who doesn't like the taste of pumpkin, don't worry, the flavor is subtle enough that these rolls go with everything. They look just like mini pumpkins and are sure to be a hit.

THE THINGS YOU'LL NEED

Pumpkin Rolls

2½ to 3 cups plus 2 tablespoons bread flour

1 teaspoon active dry yeast

¼ cup warm milk

2 teaspoons sugar

2 large eggs

½ cup canned unsweetened pumpkin puree

1½ teaspoons salt

12 tablespoons (1½ sticks) unsalted butter, at room temperature

1 tablespoon olive oil, for coating the bowl and dough

Egg wash: 1 large egg beaten with a pinch of salt

15 pecan halves, toasted

Equipment

Stand mixer fitted with the dough hook

LET'S GET STARTED!

1. In the bowl of a stand mixer, whisk together 2 tablespoons of the bread flour, the yeast, warm milk, and sugar. Set aside until foamy, about 10 minutes.

2. Once foamy, stir in the eggs and pumpkin puree.

3. Stir 1 cup of the bread flour into the yeast mixture until a thick paste forms.

4. Fit the stand mixer with the dough hook and on low speed, beat in the salt and butter. Mix until combined, 2 to 3 minutes.

5. Beat in the remaining flour ½ cup at a time, mixing well after each addition, until the dough is soft and pulls away from the sides of the bowl, 3 to 5 minutes.

6. On a lightly floured surface, knead the dough for an additional minute, then form it into a large ball. If the dough is too sticky, add more flour as needed.

7. Grease a large bowl with the olive oil and place the dough inside. Roll the dough in the oil to completely coat. Cover the bowl with a clean cloth and let rest at room temperature until doubled in size, 1 to 2 hours.

8. Preheat the oven to 350°F. Line 2 baking sheets with parchment paper and lightly grease the paper.

9. On a lightly floured surface, divide the dough into 15 portions and shape each portion into a ball. Keep the dough covered with a clean cloth to prevent a skin from forming.

10. On an unfloured surface, roll one ball of dough into a 16-inch rope.

• CONTINUES •

11. With the rope, create a loop with a 5-inch tail and a 2-inch tail Ⓐ.
12. Weave the 5-inch tail around the loop Ⓑ.
13. Hold the end of the 5-inch tail in place and weave the 2-inch tail into the loop Ⓒ. Tightly pinch the ends together Ⓓ.
14. Place the roll seam side down 2 inches apart on the baking sheets. Repeat with the remaining dough.
15. Cover with a clean cloth and let rest for 10 minutes.
16. Brush the rolls with the egg wash.
17. Bake until golden brown, 20 to 25 minutes.
18. Place a toasted pecan in the center of each roll for the stem, then let cool for 5 minutes on the baking sheets.

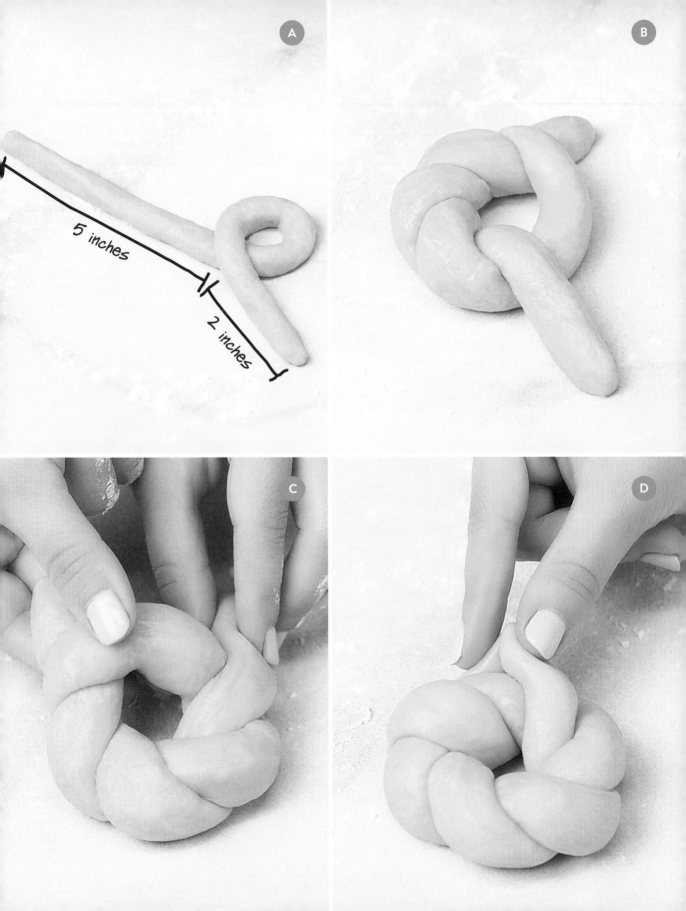

5 inches

2 inches

CHAPTER EIGHT

CHRISTMAS

REINDEER CAKE

'Tis the season! This is the kind of cake that brings back so many wonderful memories of spending Christmas with my family. During the holidays, I used to dress up as Santa and my sister would be a reindeer. To this day, we still laugh about how we used to run around the house pretending to deliver presents. A traditional spice cake is a welcome addition to any festive feast or holiday party. Not only is this recipe delicious, it's also super cute.

THE THINGS YOU'LL NEED

Fondant
Fondant: brown, dark brown, cream, black, white, green, and red

Spice Cake
1½ cups cake flour
1½ cups all-purpose flour
1 teaspoon baking powder
1 teaspoon baking soda
½ teaspoon salt
2 teaspoons ground cinnamon
1 teaspoon ground cloves
1 teaspoon ground ginger
1 teaspoon ground nutmeg
2 sticks (8 ounces) unsalted butter, at room temperature
1 cup packed light brown sugar
¾ cup granulated sugar
¼ cup honey
4 large eggs
2 teaspoons vanilla extract
1 cup buttermilk

Decorations
2 batches Swiss Buttercream Frosting (page 17)
Brown food coloring
Edible white candy pearls
1 round chocolate candy (Milk Dud)

Equipment
Teardrop cookie cutters: 1¾ inch and 2½ inch (templates on page 249)
Antler template (page 249)
Eye template (page 248)
Holly leaf template (page 248)
Decorating tips: Two #824, #4B, #2A

FONDANT PREP!

1. Work with fondant on wax paper sprinkled with powdered sugar.
2. For the antlers, roll out the brown fondant to ⅛ inch thick. Cut out 2 antlers using the template **A**.
3. For the ears, roll out the dark brown and cream fondant to ⅛ inch thick. Use the teardrop cookie cutters to cut 2 large dark brown outer ears and 2 small cream inner ears. Using water, attach the small teardrops to the large teardrops **B**.
4. For the eyes, roll out the black fondant to ¼ inch thick. Cut out 2 eyes using the template. Roll 2 small balls of white fondant for the eye reflection and attach to the eyes.
5. For the holly, roll out the green fondant to ¼ inch thick. Cut out holly leaves using the template. Use a fondant tool or toothpick to make leaf details **C**. Roll ¼-inch balls of red fondant for the holly berries.
6. Set aside to harden for about 24 hours. Once dry, the antlers should stand upright without bending.

LET'S GET STARTED!

1. Preheat the oven to 350°F. Grease three 6-inch round cake pans and line the bottoms with rounds of parchment paper.
2. In a medium bowl, whisk together the cake flour, all-purpose flour, baking powder, baking soda, salt, cinnamon, cloves, ginger, and nutmeg.
3. In a large bowl, with an electric mixer, beat the butter, brown sugar, granulated sugar, and honey until light and fluffy, 3 to 5 minutes.
4. Add the eggs one at a time, beating well after each addition.
5. Beat in the vanilla.

• CONTINUES •

6. On low speed, alternate adding the flour mixture and the buttermilk to the butter mixture, beginning and ending with the flour mixture.

7. Divide the batter evenly among the prepared pans and bake until a wooden pick inserted into the center comes out clean, 40 to 42 minutes.

8. Let cool in the pans for 15 minutes, then turn out onto a wire rack to cool completely.

9. Level off the tops with a cake leveler or a large serrated knife to create three 2-inch cake layers.

TIME TO DECORATE!

1. Make the Swiss Buttercream Frosting. Tint half the frosting light brown.

2. Stack the cake layers on top of one another with a thin layer of light brown frosting in between the layers. Frost the entire cake with light brown frosting.

3. Divide the remaining frosting among 3 bowls **D**:

    Bowl 1: Tint light brown and scoop into a decorating bag fitted with a #824 tip.

    Bowl 2: Tint dark brown and scoop into separate decorating bags fitted with a #824 tip and a #4B tip.

    Bowl 3: Leave untinted and scoop into a decorating bag fitted with a #2A tip.

    Pipe the frostings on top of the cake for decoration.

4. Place the fondant decorations on the cake: antlers, ears, eyes, and holly.

5. Sprinkle pearls on top.

6. Place the Milk Dud on for the nose.

MELTED SNOWMAN BARK

MAKES 12 PIECES

Oh no! These snowmen stayed out in the sun a little too long and melted. Thankfully for us, they are made out of delicious chocolate and peppermint. This recipe is so simple to make that everyone of all ages can help out with the decorating. Running short on time? They only take a few minutes to make and are a perfect last-minute gift.

THE THINGS YOU'LL NEED

Peppermint Bark

1 cup white chocolate chips
(Nestlé)
1 cup bright white Candy Melts
(Wilton)
¼ cup finely crushed peppermint
candies

Decorations

6 mini peanut butter cups
(Reese's), cut in half
24 small eye candies (Wilton)
12 orange sprinkles
6 pretzel sticks (Snyder's), cut into
quarters
36 red chip crunch sprinkles
(Wilton)

LET'S GET STARTED!

1. Line a baking sheet with wax paper.
2. Melt the white chocolate chips and Candy Melts together until smooth.
3. Fold in the crushed peppermint candy.
4. Spread evenly onto the baking sheet.

TIME TO DECORATE!

1. While the chocolate is still wet, place the candies to create snowmen: 1 peanut butter cup half for the hat, 2 eye candies for the eyes, 1 orange sprinkle for the nose, 2 pretzels for the arms, and 3 red chips for the buttons.
2. Allow the bark to set for about 30 minutes at room temperature.
3. Cut the bark into 12 "melted snowman" pieces.

· RO **TIP** ·

To set the bark faster,
chill in the refrigerator for
15 minutes.

GINGERBREAD MAN COOKIES

MAKES 2 DOZEN COOKIES

Making Gingerbread Man Cookies is my favorite holiday tradition and this recipe is the best I've ever had. Every time I make a batch of them they are devoured by everyone within an hour. They have all of the classic gingerbread flavor, but are more soft and chewy.

THE THINGS YOU'LL NEED

Gingerbread Dough
4 cups all-purpose flour
1 teaspoon baking soda
2 teaspoons ground cinnamon
1½ teaspoons ground ginger
½ teaspoon ground cloves
½ teaspoon ground nutmeg
1 teaspoon salt
12 tablespoons (1½ sticks) unsalted butter, at room temperature
1 cup packed dark brown sugar
1 large egg
¾ cup molasses

Decorations
Round red cinnamon candies (Red Hots)
1 batch Royal Icing (page 16)

Equipment
Gingerbread man cookie cutter (template on page 249)
#3 decorating tip

LET'S GET STARTED!

1. In a medium bowl, whisk together the flour, baking soda, cinnamon, ginger, cloves, nutmeg, and salt.
2. In a large bowl, with an electric mixer, beat the butter and brown sugar until light and fluffy, 3 to 5 minutes.
3. Mix in the egg and molasses.
4. On low speed, mix in half the flour mixture, then repeat until well combined.
5. Shape the dough into a disk and wrap in plastic wrap. Refrigerate for 3 hours.
6. Preheat the oven to 350°F. Line 2 baking sheets with parchment paper.
7. On a lightly floured surface, roll out the dough to a ¼-inch thickness. Cut out gingerbread men using the cookie cutter and place them 1 inch apart on the baking sheets.
8. Freeze the cookies for 15 minutes.
9. Bake until the cookies are firm to the touch and look dry, about 10 minutes.
10. While the cookies are still warm, gently press 3 Red Hots down the center for buttons.
11. Let cool on the baking sheets for 2 minutes, then transfer to a wire rack to cool completely.

TIME TO DECORATE!

1. Make the Royal Icing and scoop into a decorating bag fitted with a #3 tip.
2. Pipe eyes, mouths, and trim details onto the gingerbread men.

CHRISTMAS TREE
CUPCAKES

Pine-ing fir a treemendously good cupcake this holiday season? You might not think coconut and eggnog go together, but their flavor combination is a Christmas miracle.

THE THINGS YOU'LL NEED

Eggnog Cake
1 cup all-purpose flour
½ cup cake flour
1 cup sugar
1½ teaspoons baking powder
¼ teaspoon salt
1 teaspoon ground cinnamon
½ teaspoon ground nutmeg
3 large egg yolks
1 teaspoon rum extract
1 teaspoon vanilla extract
2 tablespoons vegetable oil
¾ cup half-and-half
8 tablespoons (1 stick) unsalted
   butter, cut into cubes and chilled

Decorations
1 bag (12 ounces) green Candy
   Melts (Wilton)
12 pretzel sticks (Snyder's)
Rainbow confetti sprinkles
Yellow star sprinkles
1 batch Swiss Buttercream Frosting
   (page 17)
1 cup sweetened shredded coconut

Equipment
Stand mixer fitted with the paddle
   attachment
Decorating tips: #4, #809

LET'S GET STARTED!

1. Preheat the oven to 375°F. Line 12 cups of a muffin tin with brown paper liners.
2. In a stand mixer fitted with the paddle attachment, mix together the all-purpose flour, cake flour, sugar, baking powder, salt, cinnamon, and nutmeg.
3. In a small bowl, whisk together the egg yolks, rum extract, vanilla, oil, and half-and-half.
4. On low speed, add the cold butter to the dry ingredients and mix until a soft, pebbly texture forms.
5. On low speed, add the half-and-half mixture in thirds, mixing well after each addition until the batter is smooth.
6. Fill the paper liners two-thirds full with the batter. Bake until a wooden pick inserted into the center of a cupcake comes out clean, 15 to 19 minutes.

TIME TO DECORATE!

1. Melt the green Candy Melts and scoop into a decorating bag fitted with a #4 tip.
2. Line a baking sheet with wax paper and place the pretzel sticks about 3 inches apart. Pipe the green candy back and forth across each pretzel stick to create a Christmas tree, leaving the bottom third uncovered to be the trunk.
3. When still wet, sprinkle with rainbow confetti for decoration and top with a star sprinkle.
4. Freeze the trees for 10 minutes to set.
5. Make the Swiss Buttercream Frosting. Scoop it into a decorating bag fitted with a #809 tip. Pour the shredded coconut into a bowl.
6. Pipe a mound of frosting onto the center of each cupcake. Roll the frosting in the sweetened shredded coconut for snow.
7. Place a candy tree in the center of each cupcake.

WOVEN STOCKING COOKIES

MAKES 8 TO 10 COOKIES

Santa Claus is coming to town . . . So let's make him cookies he'll never forget! If you're feeling crafty this year, these cookies are made by weaving together thin strips of cookie dough. You can even customize them by icing names on the top. With a little patience and determination you'll have the most memorable sweet treats this holiday season.

THE THINGS YOU'LL NEED

Peppermint Cookies
4 large egg yolks
½ cup heavy cream
4 teaspoons peppermint extract
4½ cups all-purpose flour
¼ cup cornstarch
1 teaspoon salt
1½ cups sugar
3 sticks (12 ounces) unsalted
    butter, at room temperature
1 teaspoon red food coloring gel
1 teaspoon green food coloring gel

Decorations
1 batch Swiss Buttercream Frosting
    (page 17)
White sanding sugar

Equipment
Stocking cookie cutter (template
    on page 251)

LET'S GET STARTED!

1. In a small bowl, whisk the egg yolks, cream, and peppermint extract until smooth.
2. In a large bowl, with an electric mixer, mix the flour, cornstarch, salt, sugar, and butter until the mixture resembles coarse meal.
3. On low speed, slowly mix in the cream mixture until the dough holds together when pinched.
4. Divide the dough into 2 equal portions. Tint one portion red and the other green.
5. Shape each portion into a disk and wrap separately in plastic wrap. Refrigerate for 1 hour.
6. Preheat the oven to 350°F. Line 2 baking sheets with parchment paper.
7. On a lightly floured surface, divide the red and green dough into 5 portions each.
8. Roll out one red and one green portion of dough to a ¼-inch thickness. Cut into strips 5 inches long and ½ inch wide.

• CONTINUES •

9. On a flat surface lined with parchment paper, weave the strips together  A . Repeat with the remaining dough to make 5 woven grids.
10. Cut out stockings using the cookie cutter B . Place the cookies 2 inches apart on the baking sheets C .
11. Freeze the cookies for 15 minutes.
12. Bake until the cookies are firm to the touch but not browned at the edges, about 10 minutes.
13. Let cool on the baking sheets for 2 minutes, then transfer to a wire rack to cool completely.

TIME TO DECORATE!

1. Make the Swiss Buttercream Frosting.
2. Spread the frosting over the top of the cookies for the stocking tops. Sprinkle the sanding sugar over the frosting D .

▶ RO **TIP** ◀

I like to make 5 WOVEN GRIDS
because the dough is more
manageable in small sizes, but feel
free to make larger grids.

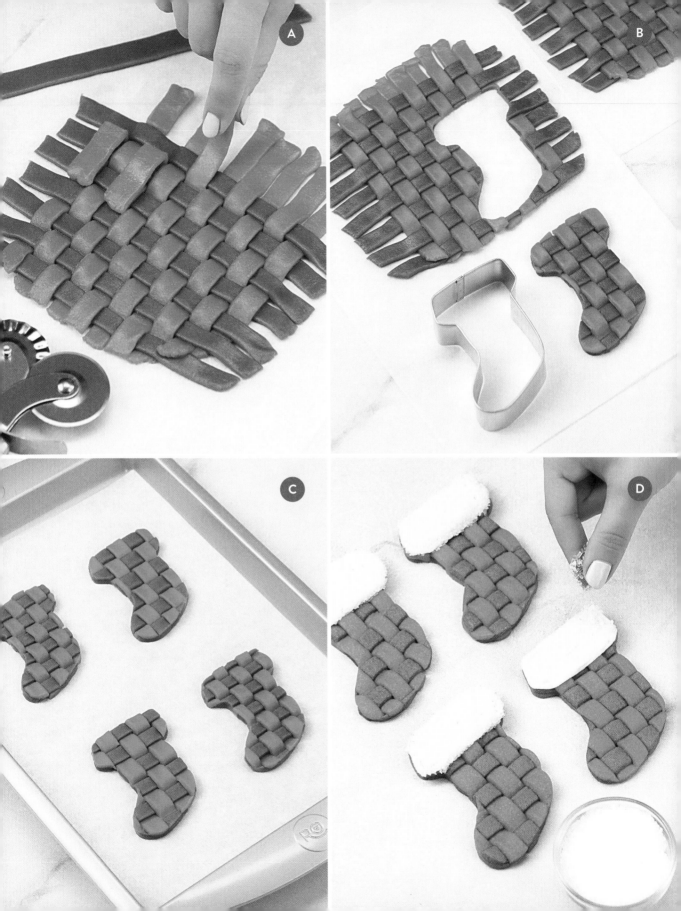

POLAR BEAR PAWS

— MAKES 2 DOZEN CANDIES —

With gooey caramel and roasted peanuts in the middle and a white chocolate coating on the outside, it's no wonder Polar Bear Paw candies are a timeless winter staple. I like to keep the decorations simple to look like actual bear paws. They are pawsitively delicious.

THE THINGS YOU'LL NEED

Peanut Caramel
¾ cup plus ¼ cup heavy cream
¾ cup granulated sugar
¼ cup packed light brown sugar
¼ cup honey
2 tablespoons light corn syrup
1 teaspoon lemon juice
2 tablespoons unsalted butter
½ teaspoon salt
½ teaspoon vanilla extract
2 cups unsalted roasted peanuts

Decorations
4 cups white chocolate coating
   wafers (Ghirardelli)
½ cup dark chocolate coating
   wafers (Ghirardelli)

Equipment
Medium heavy-bottomed saucepan
   (do not use a nonstick pan)
Candy thermometer
#2 decorating tip

LET'S GET STARTED!

1. Line a baking sheet with parchment paper and grease the paper.
2. Make the peanut caramel: In a medium heavy-bottomed saucepan fitted with a candy thermometer, whisk together ¾ cup of the heavy cream, the granulated sugar, brown sugar, honey, corn syrup, lemon juice, and butter.
3. Bring to a boil over medium heat and cook until the temperature reaches 265°F. Stir every few minutes with a silicone spatula. Remove the pan from the heat. Slowly whisk in the remaining ¼ cup heavy cream.
4. Stir in the salt, vanilla, and peanuts.
5. Pour the caramel mixture onto the prepared baking sheet and spread evenly. Let cool for 15 minutes. Refrigerate for 10 minutes to chill.
6. Line a baking sheet with wax paper. Scoop 1 tablespoon of the caramel and form it into a paw shape. Place the shaped caramel on the baking sheet.

TIME TO DECORATE!

1. Melt the white chocolate. Dip the caramels into the melted chocolate to cover completely.
2. Return the caramels to the lined baking sheet. If desired, dip the covered caramels again.
3. Let set completely before decorating, about 15 minutes.
4. Melt the dark chocolate and scoop into a decorating bag fitted with a #2 tip. Pipe paw prints onto each caramel.

PEPPERMINT
LOLLIPOP COOKIES

MAKES 16 COOKIES

Put a fun twist on your holiday baking by making cookie pops that look and taste like peppermint lollipops!
It's the most wonderful time of the year . . . for cookies!

THE THINGS YOU'LL NEED

Peppermint Cookies

2 cups all-purpose flour

½ teaspoon salt

2 sticks (8 ounces) unsalted butter, at room temperature

½ cup granulated sugar

¼ cup powdered sugar

2 large egg yolks

2 teaspoons peppermint extract

½ teaspoon red food coloring gel

Equipment

Sixteen 8-inch lollipop sticks

LET'S GET STARTED!

1. In a medium bowl, whisk together the flour and salt.
2. In a large bowl, with an electric mixer, beat the butter, granulated sugar, and powdered sugar until light and fluffy, 3 to 5 minutes.
3. Add the egg yolks one at a time, beating well after each addition.
4. Beat in the peppermint extract.
5. On low speed, beat in the flour mixture until combined.
6. Divide the dough into 2 equal portions. Tint one portion with red food coloring. Leave the other portion untinted.
7. Shape the dough into disks and wrap separately with plastic wrap. Refrigerate for at least 3 hours.
8. Preheat the oven to 350°F. Line 3 baking sheets with parchment paper.
9. Divide each disk of dough into 16 equal portions. Roll each portion of dough into a 5-inch rope.
10. Twist one red and one untinted rope together and roll into a 12-inch rope. Coil the rope into a round cookie and place 2 inches apart on a baking sheet. Repeat.
11. Insert a lollipop stick halfway into each cookie.
12. Freeze the cookies for 10 minutes.
13. Bake until the cookies are firm to the touch but not browned at the edges, 13 to 14 minutes.
14. Let cool on the baking sheets for 2 minutes, then transfer to a wire rack to cool completely.

PEANUT BUTTER
PINECONES

The coming together of chocolate and peanut butter is a joyful occasion worth celebrating. So why not throw a party featuring these no-bake goodies? With a creamy filling on the inside and crunchy chocolate-coated cereal on the outside you'll be sure to have a holly jolly Christmas.

THE THINGS YOU'LL NEED

Peanut Butter Chocolate Treats
¼ cup chocolate chips
1½ teaspoons coconut oil
1 cup cornflakes
½ cup unsweetened cocoa powder
5 tablespoons powdered sugar, sifted
3 tablespoons peanut butter
1 teaspoon unsalted butter, at room temperature
¼ teaspoon salt

Decorations
10 gluten-free pretzel sticks (Snyder's)
1 cup powdered sugar

LET'S GET STARTED!

1. Line a baking sheet with parchment paper.
2. In a large bowl, melt the chocolate and coconut oil together. Gently mix together the chocolate mixture and cornflakes, being careful not to break the cornflakes.
3. Add the cocoa powder and mix until every cornflake is coated. Spread evenly over the baking sheet and refrigerate for 10 minutes.
4. In a medium bowl, mix the 5 tablespoons powdered sugar and peanut butter. Mix in the butter and salt until combined.
5. Line a baking sheet with wax paper. Roll 1 teaspoon of the peanut butter mixture into a ball and place on the baking sheet. Repeat to form 10 balls. Set aside the remaining peanut butter mixture for decoration.

TIME TO DECORATE!

1. Insert a pretzel stick into a peanut butter ball and shape into a pinecone that reaches halfway up the pretzel stick. Use the top half of the pretzel for control while decorating.
2. Place pieces of the cornflakes into the peanut butter cone to form the scales of a pinecone. If the peanut butter gets too soft to work with, chill for 10 minutes.
3. Once the cone is fully covered in cornflakes, cut the top of the pretzel to the height of the pinecone. Cover the cut end of the pretzel with some of the remaining peanut butter mixture.
4. Lightly dust the pinecones with powdered sugar to look like snow.

RED VELVET
SANTA BROWNIES

These brownies are dedicated to my dad, who for twenty years would dress up like Santa and volunteer his time at hospitals and community events to help spread holiday cheer. Red velvet brownies are so good, you'll want to have them every Christmas.

THE THINGS YOU'LL NEED

Red Velvet Brownies
1½ cups gluten-free 1-to-1 baking flour (Bob's Red Mill)
2 teaspoons unsweetened cocoa powder
Pinch of salt
3 large eggs
2 cups sugar
1 teaspoon vanilla extract
2 tablespoons distilled white vinegar
1 tablespoon red food coloring
12 tablespoons (1½ sticks) unsalted butter
6 ounces dark chocolate, chopped

Decorations
1 batch Royal Icing (page 16)
Food coloring: black and gold
1 batch Swiss Buttercream Frosting (page 17)
Chocolate crisp pearls (Valrhona)

Equipment
Decorating tips: #1, #2, #30

LET'S GET STARTED!

1. Preheat the oven to 325°F. Grease a 9 x 13-inch baking pan and line the bottom and sides of the pan with parchment paper. Grease the parchment paper.
2. In a small bowl, whisk together the gluten-free flour, cocoa powder, and salt.
3. In a large bowl, whisk together the eggs, sugar, vanilla, vinegar, and food coloring.
4. Melt the butter and chocolate together and mix until smooth. Whisk the sugar mixture into the chocolate mixture until well combined.
5. Mix in the flour mixture just until no streaks of flour remain (do not overmix).
6. Pour the batter into the prepared pan and bake until a wooden pick inserted into the center comes out clean, about 45 minutes.
7. Let the brownies cool in the pan, then cut into 12 rectangles.

TIME TO DECORATE!

1. Make the Royal Icing. Divide it between 2 bowls. Tint one bowl black and the other bowl gold. Scoop the black icing into a decorating bag fitted with a #2 tip and the gold icing into a bag fitted with a #1 tip.
2. Pipe the black icing onto the bottom part of the brownie to create a belt. Let the icing harden for about 30 minutes.
3. Pipe the gold icing onto the middle of the belt for the buckle.
4. Make the Swiss Buttercream Frosting. Scoop it into a decorating bag fitted with a #30 tip. Pipe coat trim details.
5. Place the pearls on the frosting for buttons.

SNOWBALL COOKIES

MAKES 2 DOZEN COOKIES

A holiday classic, snowball cookies are simple to make and beloved by many. They melt in your mouth and are even better paired with a warm holiday drink, such as hot cocoa or apple cider. It doesn't have to be snowing outside to enjoy these crumbly and delicate treats rolled in powdered sugar.

THE THINGS YOU'LL NEED

Pecan Cookies
1½ cups all-purpose flour
1 cup finely chopped toasted
   pecans
Pinch of salt
8 tablespoons (1 stick) unsalted
   butter, at room temperature
¼ cup granulated sugar
¼ cup powdered sugar
Seeds of ½ vanilla bean
½ teaspoon vanilla extract

Decoration 2 to 3 cups powdered
   sugar, sifted

LET'S GET STARTED!

1. Preheat the oven to 350°F. Line 2 baking sheets with parchment paper.
2. In a medium bowl, whisk together the flour, pecans, and salt.
3. In a large bowl, with an electric mixer, beat the butter, granulated sugar, and powdered sugar until light and fluffy, 3 to 5 minutes.
4. Beat in the vanilla seeds and vanilla extract.
5. On low speed, beat in the flour mixture until combined.
6. Roll 2 tablespoons of dough into a ball and place on a baking sheet, spacing them 1 inch apart.
7. Bake until the bottoms of the cookies start to turn golden brown, about 12 minutes.
8. Let cool on the baking sheets for 5 minutes.

TIME TO DECORATE!

1. While the cookies are still warm, roll them in the powdered sugar.
2. Let cool for 10 minutes, then roll again.

NEW YEAR'S EVE

CHAMPAGNE CUPCAKES

MAKES 12 CUPCAKES

Ring in the New Year with close friends and these Champagne Cupcakes. This bubbly recipe infuses champagne in both the batter and frosting to create a satisfying flavor. Cheers!

THE THINGS YOU'LL NEED

Champagne Cupcakes
¾ cup cake flour
¾ cup all-purpose flour
1¼ teaspoons baking powder
½ teaspoon salt
2 sticks (8 ounces) unsalted butter, at room temperature
1 cup granulated sugar
2 large eggs
¼ teaspoon almond extract
½ cup flat champagne (no carbonation)

Decorations
1 batch Champagne Frosting (page 18)
Coarse gold sanding sugar

Equipment
Gold foil liners
#1M decorating tip

LET'S GET STARTED!

1. Preheat the oven to 350°F. Line 12 cups of a muffin tin with gold foil liners.
2. In a medium bowl, whisk together the cake flour, all-purpose flour, baking powder, and salt.
3. In a large bowl, with an electric mixer, beat the butter and granulated sugar until light and fluffy, 3 to 5 minutes.
4. Add the eggs one at a time, beating well after each addition.
5. Beat in the almond extract.
6. On low speed, alternate adding the flour mixture and champagne to the butter mixture, beginning and ending with the flour mixture.
7. Fill each paper liner two-thirds full with the batter. Bake until a wooden pick inserted into the center of a cupcake comes out clean, 14 to 16 minutes.
8. Transfer to a wire rack to cool.

TIME TO DECORATE!

1. Make the Champagne Frosting. Scoop it into a decorating bag fitted with a #1M tip and frost the cupcakes.
2. Sprinkle the frosting with gold sanding sugar.

SNOWY STAR BEIGNETS

MAKES 3 TO 4 DOZEN BEIGNETS

Yay for beignets! The first time I tasted these light fluffy pastries was at Disneyland. They were so good I taught myself how to make them from scratch. If you like donuts, you'll love beignets, which are best served hot and fresh. They'll be the star of your New Year's party.

THE THINGS YOU'LL NEED

Beignets
1 envelope (¼ ounce) active dry yeast
1½ cups warm water
12 tablespoons granulated sugar
2 large eggs
1 teaspoon vanilla extract
1 cup buttermilk
3½ cups bread flour
4 tablespoons vegetable shortening
1 teaspoon salt
4 cups all-purpose flour, plus more as needed
1 tablespoon oil, for coating the bowl and dough
About 8 cups vegetable oil, for deep-frying

Decoration
3 cups powdered sugar

Equipment
Stand mixer fitted with the dough hook
Large heavy-bottomed pot
Candy thermometer
3-inch star cookie cutter (template on page 248)

LET'S GET STARTED!

1. In the bowl of a stand mixer, whisk together the yeast, warm water, and 2 tablespoons of the granulated sugar. Set aside until foamy, about 10 minutes.
2. Mix in the remaining 10 tablespoons granulated sugar, the eggs, vanilla, and buttermilk.
3. Stir the bread flour, shortening, and salt into the yeast mixture until a thick paste forms.
4. With the mixer on low speed, add the all-purpose flour ½ cup at a time. Mix until the dough is soft and pulls away from the sides of the bowl, 3 to 5 minutes.
5. On a lightly floured surface, knead for an additional minute and form it into a large ball. If the dough is too sticky, add more flour as needed.
6. Grease a large bowl with the oil and add the dough. Roll the dough in the oil to completely coat. Cover the bowl with a clean cloth and let rest at room temperature until doubled in size, 1 to 2 hours.
7. Pour 4 inches of oil into a large heavy-bottomed pot fitted with a candy thermometer. Heat the oil over medium heat to 350°F.
8. On a lightly floured surface, roll out the dough to a ½-inch thickness. Cut out beignets with the star cookie cutter.
9. Line a baking sheet with paper towels. Working in batches of a few at a time, fry the beignets until golden brown, 1 to 2 minutes per side. Drain the beignets on the paper towels.

TIME TO DECORATE!

1. Sift powdered sugar over the beignets.

STRAWBERRY CHAMPAGNE
MACARONS

MAKES 2 DOZEN MACARONS

Scrumptious, fancy, and refreshing! These elegant macaron confections are a wonderful way to celebrate new beginnings by pairing together two classic flavors.

THE THINGS YOU'LL NEED

Strawberry Macarons

¾ cup powdered sugar
½ cup plus 2 tablespoons almond meal
2 large egg whites, at room temperature
¼ cup granulated sugar
¼ teaspoon strawberry extract
2 drops pink food coloring gel
Pinch of salt
Edible gold stars (Wilton)

Filling

1 batch Champagne Frosting (page 18)

Equipment

1½-inch round cookie cutter (template on page 251)
Decorating tips: #2A, #21

LET'S GET STARTED!

1. Line a baking sheet with parchment paper. Trace 1½-inch-diameter circles 1 inch apart on the parchment paper, then flip the paper over. Place another baking sheet underneath the first so it is double-panned (this will help create the rough-looking layer called the "foot" of the cookie).
2. Sift the powdered sugar and almond meal into a large bowl. Whisk together to combine.
3. In a large bowl, with an electric mixer, beat the egg whites on medium speed until frothy, about 1 minute. On medium-high speed, slowly add the granulated sugar and beat until stiff peaks form, about 5 minutes.
4. Mix in the strawberry extract, food coloring, and salt until well combined.
5. Using a spatula, fold one-third of the almond mixture into the egg white mixture, about 20 strokes. Repeat two more times.
6. Scoop the batter into a decorating bag fitted with a #2A tip. Holding the bag vertically and close to the baking sheet, pipe 1½-inch rounds onto the parchment paper. Tap the baking sheet to release any air bubbles.
7. Sprinkle edible stars over the top of half the macarons.
8. Let sit for 30 minutes at room temperature to develop a skin.
9. Preheat the oven to 325°F.
10. Bake the cookies until they have puffed up and look dry (they should not brown), 13 to 16 minutes. Switch the pans from top to bottom and rotate them front to back halfway through.
11. Let cool completely on the pans.

TIME TO DECORATE!

1. Make the Champagne Frosting and scoop it into a decorating bag fitted with a #21 tip.
2. Turn the macarons without stars upside down. Pipe on a rosette of frosting, then top with a star-topped macaron.

COUNTDOWN
COOKIE POPS

Whether I'm hosting my own New Year's party or attending someone else's, I like to make these flavorsome vegan lemon zest cookie pops. The hands on the clock are about to strike twelve, but you don't have to wait until midnight to enjoy them.

THE THINGS YOU'LL NEED

Vegan Lemon Cookies

2 cups all-purpose flour
¼ teaspoon salt
¾ cup vegan butter
½ cup granulated sugar
1 teaspoon grated lemon zest
1 tablespoon lemon juice

Decorations

1 batch Vegan Royal Icing (page 16)
Vegan black food coloring
Coarse gold sanding sugar
Edible gold candy pearls

Equipment

2¼-inch round cookie cutter
   (template on page 251)
12 lollipop sticks
Decorating tips: #1, #3

LET'S GET STARTED!

1. In a medium bowl, whisk together the flour and salt.
2. In a large bowl, with an electric mixer, beat the butter and granulated sugar until light and fluffy, 3 to 5 minutes.
3. Beat in the lemon zest and juice.
4. On low speed, beat in the flour mixture until combined.
5. Shape the dough into a disk and wrap in plastic wrap. Refrigerate for 1 hour.
6. Preheat the oven to 325°F. Line 2 baking sheets with parchment paper.
7. On a lightly floured surface, roll out the dough to a ½-inch thickness. Cut out 12 cookies using the round cookie cutter and place them 2 inches apart on the baking sheets.
8. Insert a lollipop stick halfway into each cookie.
9. Freeze the cookies for 10 minutes.
10. Bake until the cookies are firm to the touch but not browned at the edges, about 10 minutes.
11. Let cool on the baking sheets for 2 minutes, then transfer to a wire rack to cool completely.

TIME TO DECORATE!

1. Make the Vegan Royal Icing. Divide it between 2 bowls. Tint one bowl black and leave the other white. Scoop the black icing into a decorating bag fitted with a #1 tip and the white icing into a decorating bag fitted with a #3 tip.
2. Outline the cookies with the white icing, then fill in the centers. Let the icing harden for about 1 hour.
3. Pipe a circle of white icing at the edge of the cookies. While the icing is still wet, sprinkle on the gold sanding sugar.
4. Pipe the black icing onto the cookies to create the face and hands of a clock. While the black icing is still wet, place a gold pearl in the center of the clock.
5. Let the cookies set for 1 hour before serving.

CHAPTER TEN

SPECIAL OCCASIONS

CONFETTI
PANCAKES

Pancakes for breakfast are such a treat. Make them even more special by adding rainbow sprinkles for a fun birthday breakfast idea. These pancakes come out golden and fluffy and are exceptionally easy to make from scratch. Growing up, my mom would ask me what cake I wanted for my birthday, and without hesitation I would always say "Funfetti!" I loved the sweet simple taste and all the colors. One year she made me these pancakes for a fun twist and the idea has stuck with me ever since.

THE THINGS YOU'LL NEED

Confetti Pancakes
1¾ cups all-purpose flour
3 tablespoons sugar
1 tablespoon baking powder
1 teaspoon baking soda
½ teaspoon salt
1¾ cups buttermilk
4 tablespoons unsalted butter, melted
2 teaspoons vanilla extract
1 large egg
¼ cup rainbow sprinkles

Decorations
1 batch Whipped Cream (page 20)
Rainbow sprinkles

Equipment
#824 decorating tip

LET'S GET STARTED!

1. In a large bowl, whisk together the flour, sugar, baking powder, baking soda, and salt.
2. In a medium bowl, whisk together the buttermilk, melted butter, vanilla, and egg.
3. Make a well in the center of the flour mixture and add the wet mixture. Stir until smooth.
4. Fold in the rainbow sprinkles.
5. Allow the batter to sit and thicken for 10 minutes.
6. Place a greased nonstick skillet over medium heat. When hot, pour in ¼ cup of the batter. Cook until bubbles form in the center, about 30 seconds. Flip the pancake and cook until golden brown on the second side, about 30 seconds.
7. Repeat with the remaining batter.

TIME TO DECORATE!

1. Stack the pancakes.
2. Make the Whipped Cream and scoop it into a decorating bag fitted with a #824 tip. Pipe a swirl of whipped cream on top of the pancakes.
3. Sprinkle with rainbow sprinkles.

BIRTHDAY

MINT CHOCOLATE
DRIP CAKE

MAKES ONE 6-INCH THREE-LAYER CAKE

Calling all mint chocolate chip lovers! The cake of your dreams has arrived. My favorite ice cream flavor is hands-down mint chocolate chip; it's frequently my go-to on hot summer days. However, this wonderful flavor should not be limited to just ice cream, which is why it also makes a fantastic drip cake. Drip cakes are both fun to look at and to make. I decorated this one to look like an ice cream cone is melting on top.

BIRTHDAY

THE THINGS YOU'LL NEED

Mint Chocolate Cake
2 cups all-purpose flour
1 cup granulated sugar
1 cup packed light brown sugar
¾ cup unsweetened cocoa powder
1 teaspoon baking powder
½ teaspoon baking soda
½ teaspoon salt
1 cup buttermilk
1 cup vegetable oil
2 large eggs
2 large egg yolks
2 teaspoons peppermint extract
½ cup hot water
½ cup mini chocolate chips

Decorations
1 batch Dark Chocolate Frosting
   (page 19)
1 batch White Chocolate Glaze
   (page 21)
Mint-green food coloring
1 sugar cone (Keebler)
2 tablespoons chopped dark
   chocolate (Ghirardelli)

Equipment
#6 decorating tip

LET'S GET STARTED!

1. Preheat the oven to 325°F. Grease three 6-inch round cake pans and line the bottoms with rounds of parchment paper.
2. In a large bowl, whisk together the flour, granulated sugar, brown sugar, cocoa powder, baking powder, baking soda, and salt.
3. In a medium bowl, whisk together the buttermilk, oil, whole eggs, egg yolks, peppermint extract, and water.
4. Make a well in the center of the flour mixture and add the wet mixture. Stir just until no dry streaks of flour remain (do not overmix).
5. Gently fold in the mini chocolate chips.
6. Divide the batter evenly among the prepared pans and bake until a wooden pick inserted into the center comes out clean, 50 to 55 minutes.
7. Let cool in the pans for 15 minutes, then turn out onto a wire rack to cool completely.
8. Level off the tops with a cake leveler or a large serrated knife. Reserve the trimmings of one of the layers for decoration.

TIME TO DECORATE!

1. Make the Dark Chocolate Frosting.
2. Stack the cakes with a thin layer of chocolate frosting in between the layers. Frost the entire cake with chocolate frosting, reserving 1 teaspoon of the frosting for step 4.
3. Refrigerate the cake for 10 minutes.
4. Crumble the reserved cake trimmings into a small bowl. Mix in the reserved 1 teaspoon chocolate frosting until a dough-like mixture forms. Shape into a ball to create the scoop of ice cream.
5. Make the White Chocolate Glaze. Tint mint green and let cool for 10 minutes (until still warm but not hot).

• CONTINUES •

6. Scoop half the glaze into a decorating bag fitted with a #6 tip.
   Pipe the glaze along the top edge of the cake, allowing it to drip
   down the sides Ⓐ.
7. Fill in the center of the cake and smooth the top Ⓑ.
8. Dip the cake ball halfway into the glaze and place it in the center
   on top of the cake Ⓒ.
9. Cover the whole ball with glaze and attach the sugar cone on top Ⓓ.
10. Sprinkle the mint-green glaze with the chopped chocolate.

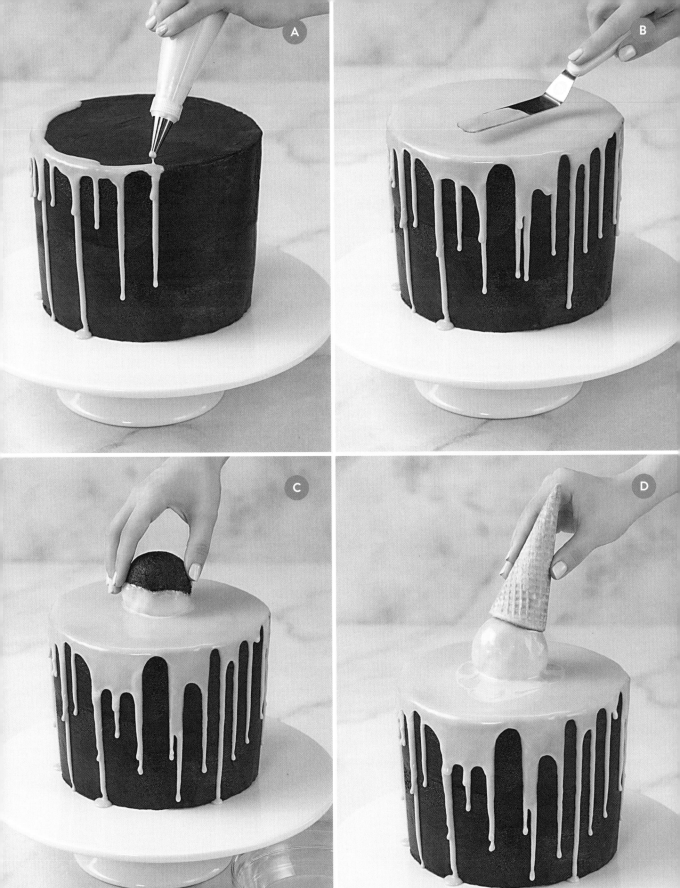

ICE CREAM CAKE

Perfect for a summertime birthday party, this cake combines cookies-and-cream ice cream with a chocolate cake. Two desserts in one is twice the fun!

THE THINGS YOU'LL NEED

Ice Cream Cake
1 gallon cookies-and-cream ice cream
1 cup all-purpose flour
½ cup granulated sugar
½ cup packed light brown sugar
⅓ cup unsweetened dark cocoa powder (Hershey's Special Dark)
1 teaspoon baking soda
½ teaspoon salt
1 large egg
½ cup sour cream
½ cup vegetable oil
1 teaspoon vanilla extract
½ cup water

Decorations
2 batches Whipped Cream (page 20)
1 cup finely crushed chocolate sandwich cookies (Oreos)
8 chocolate sandwich cookies (Oreos)

Equipment
#829 decorating tip

LET'S GET STARTED!

1. Line the inside of an 8-inch round cake pan with plastic wrap. Fill with the ice cream. Freeze until set, 3 to 4 hours.
2. Preheat the oven to 350°F. Grease an 8-inch round cake pan and line the bottom with a round of parchment paper.
3. In a large bowl, whisk together the flour, granulated sugar, brown sugar, cocoa powder, baking soda, and salt.
4. In a medium bowl, whisk together the egg, sour cream, oil, vanilla, and water.
5. Make a well in the center of the flour mixture and add the wet mixture. Stir just until no dry streaks of flour remain (do not overmix).
6. Pour the batter into the prepared pan and bake until a wooden pick inserted into the center comes out clean, about 40 minutes.
7. Let cool in the pan for 15 minutes, then turn out onto a wire rack to cool completely.
8. Level off the top of the cake with a cake leveler or a large serrated knife.
9. Stack the cake on top of the ice cream in the pan and freeze for 15 minutes.

TIME TO DECORATE!

1. Make the Whipped Cream.
2. Flip the ice cream cake out of the pan onto a serving dish, cake side down. Remove the pan and plastic wrap.
3. Frost the entire cake with whipped cream. Scoop the remaining whipped cream into a decorating bag fitted with a #829 tip.
4. Press crushed Oreos around the bottom border of the cake.
5. Pipe 8 rosettes on the top of the cake. Place an Oreo on each rosette.

PRINCESS CAKE

The classic princess cake! I first made this cake as an online tutorial video and it is now the most viewed cake video on YouTube. It's one of my favorite cakes to make because it can be customized to be any kind of princess you can imagine. Simply change the decorations to match whatever your doll of choice is. This yellow cake recipe is designed to work perfectly with the princess cake pan from my baking line. As a kid my birthdays often had a specific theme such as dinosaurs, mermaids, and princesses. Throwing themed parties is still a passion of mine to this day, which is why I often find myself returning to make this again and again.

THE THINGS YOU'LL NEED

Yellow Cake
5¼ cups cake flour
1 tablespoon baking powder
1 teaspoon salt
7 large eggs
3½ cups granulated sugar
3½ teaspoons vanilla extract
1 teaspoon lemon extract
2 sticks (8 ounces) unsalted butter, melted
1 cup whole milk, warmed
¾ cup buttermilk, warmed

Decorations
1 batch Swiss Buttercream Frosting (page 17)
Powdered sugar
2 ounces yellow fondant
24 ounces white fondant
24 ounces light blue fondant
1 batch Royal Icing (page 16)
Blue food coloring

Equipment
Princess cake pan (Ro Baking Line by Wilton)
11½-inch-tall doll (Barbie)
#2 decorating tip

LET'S GET STARTED!

1. Preheat the oven to 350°F. Grease the three princess cake pans.
2. In a medium bowl, whisk together the cake flour, baking powder, and salt.
3. In a large bowl, with an electric mixer, beat the eggs, granulated sugar, vanilla, and lemon extract until doubled in volume, 2 to 3 minutes.
4. In a small bowl, stir together the melted butter, milk, and buttermilk.
5. Mix the flour mixture into the egg mixture until well combined, then whisk in the milk mixture until smooth.
6. Fill each pan two-thirds full with batter (using about 3½ cups per pan) **A** and bake until a wooden pick inserted into the center comes out clean, 35 to 40 minutes.
7. Let cool in the pans for 15 minutes, then turn out of the pans onto a wire rack to cool completely.
8. Level off the top of each cake with a cake leveler or a large serrated knife **B**.

TIME TO DECORATE!

1. Make the Swiss Buttercream Frosting.
2. Stack the cakes in ascending order, leveled side down, with a thin layer of frosting in between the cake layers **C**.
3. Crumb coat the cake **D**. Refrigerate for 30 minutes to set.
4. Make the crown: On a flat surface sprinkled with powdered sugar, roll out the yellow fondant to ¼ inch thick. Cut into a crown shape and curve it to fit the doll's head. Once shaped, let dry until hardened.
5. Make the dress: On a flat surface sprinkled with powdered sugar, roll out the white fondant to a 16-inch round, ¼ inch thick.

• CONTINUES •

6. Drape the white fondant over the cake and form ruffles in the front of the dress. Smooth the fondant and cut away any excess around the bottom. Cut a small round opening in the fondant to match the opening at the top of the cake (where you will insert the doll).

7. On a flat surface sprinkled with powdered sugar, roll out the light blue fondant to a 16-inch round, ¼ inch thick.

8. Place the light blue fondant over the white fondant. Using a small knife, carefully cut out a triangular panel from the front to show the white ruffles. Do not cut into the white fondant. Gently remove the panel and save for step 10. Smooth the fondant and cut away any excess around the bottom. Cut a small round in the fondant to match the opening at the top of the cake (where you will insert the doll).

9. Wrap the doll's lower half in food-safe plastic wrap to protect the doll and cake.

10. Using the reserved piece of light blue fondant, form a dress bodice around the doll's torso. Cut a strip of fondant ½ inch wide and 5 inches long for the waist sash.

11. Insert the doll into the center of the cake. Wrap the fondant sash around the waist, using water as an adhesive.

12. Make the Royal Icing. Tint light blue and scoop into a decorating bag fitted with a #2 tip.

13. Pipe decorative details on the light blue fondant along the trim of the dress.

14. Place the crown on the doll's head.

DONUT CAKE

It's a cake recipe that both looks and tastes like a donut. Inspired by old-fashioned donuts, which have a cakey consistency and exemplary flavor. Sounds pretty good, donut?

THE THINGS YOU'LL NEED

Donut Cake
1½ cups all-purpose flour
1 cup cake flour
1 cup sugar
3½ teaspoons baking powder
½ teaspoon ground cinnamon
1½ teaspoons salt
1 cup buttermilk
2 large eggs
1½ teaspoons vanilla extract
2 tablespoons unsalted butter, melted

Decorations
1 batch Swiss Buttercream Frosting (page 17)
Food coloring: brown and pink
Rainbow sprinkles

Equipment
Two 8-inch ring pans
#12 decorating tip

LET'S GET STARTED!

1. Preheat the oven to 325°F. Grease two 8-inch ring pans.
2. In a large bowl, whisk together the all-purpose flour, cake flour, sugar, baking powder, cinnamon, and salt.
3. In a medium bowl, whisk together the buttermilk, eggs, vanilla, and melted butter.
4. Make a well in the center of the flour mixture and add the wet mixture. Stir just until no dry streaks of flour remain (do not overmix).
5. Divide the batter evenly between the prepared pans and bake until a wooden pick inserted into the center comes out clean, 18 to 20 minutes.
6. Let cool in the pans for 15 minutes, then turn the cakes out onto a wire rack to cool completely.
7. Level off the top of each cake with a cake leveler or a large serrated knife.

TIME TO DECORATE!

1. Make the Swiss Buttercream Frosting. Divide it between 2 bowls. Tint one bowl light brown and the other pink.
2. Stack the cakes leveled sides together, with a thin layer of brown frosting in between, to form a donut. Frost the entire cake with light brown frosting.
3. Scoop the pink frosting into a decorating bag fitted with a #12 tip. Pipe a wavy donut glaze outline around the top of the cake and fill. Use a spatula to smooth.
4. Top with rainbow sprinkles.

CHALKBOARD
COOKIES

Chalk-full of cinnamon goodness these classic chalkboard back-to-school cookies are vegan and make a thoughtful gift for friends or your favorite teacher.

THE THINGS YOU'LL NEED

Vegan Cinnamon Cookies
1¾ cups all-purpose flour
¼ teaspoon salt
1 teaspoon ground cinnamon
¾ cup vegan butter
¾ cup powdered sugar

Decorations
1 batch Vegan Royal Icing (page 16)
Food coloring: brown, red, green, and white (TruColor)
Vegan black fondant (Satin Ice)

Equipment
3 x 2-inch rectangle cookie cutter (template on page 249)
Three #2 decorating tips
Small paintbrush

LET'S GET STARTED!

1. In a medium bowl, whisk together the flour, salt, and cinnamon.
2. In a large bowl, with an electric mixer, beat the vegan butter and powdered sugar until light and fluffy, 3 to 5 minutes.
3. On low speed, beat in the flour mixture until combined.
4. Shape the dough into a disk and wrap in plastic wrap. Refrigerate for at least 1 hour.
5. Preheat the oven to 325°F. Line 2 baking sheets with parchment paper.
6. On a lightly floured surface, roll out the dough to ¼ inch thick. Cut out cookies using the rectangle cookie cutter and place them 1 inch apart on the baking sheets.
7. Bake until the cookies are firm to the touch but not browned at the edges, 10 to 12 minutes.
8. Let cool on the baking sheets for 2 minutes, then transfer to a wire rack to cool completely.

TIME TO DECORATE!

1. Make the Vegan Royal Icing. Divide it among 3 bowls. Tint one bowl brown, one red, and one green. Scoop into separate decorating bags fitted with #2 tips.
2. On wax paper sprinkled with powdered sugar, roll out the black fondant to ⅛ inch thick and cut out rectangles using the cookie cutter.
3. Using the royal icing, attach the fondant rectangles onto each cookie.
4. Using a small paintbrush with white food coloring, write messages on the cookies.
5. Pipe the brown icing around the edge to create a border.
6. Pipe the red and green icing to make apples.

GRADUATION/SCHOOL

BLUEBERRY PANCAKE
MUFFINS

Pancake, meet Muffin. School starting up again means the return of early mornings. For days when there just isn't time to make a full breakfast, these muffins are the perfect answer. Bake ahead of time and keep them in the fridge for up to a week (or freeze for up to a month), then grab them and go in the morning. They have all the flavor of a blueberry pancake with the texture of a muffin, and are especially good reheated in the microwave.

THE THINGS YOU'LL NEED

Blueberry Muffins
1½ cups all-purpose flour
¼ cup sugar
1 tablespoon baking powder
1 teaspoon baking soda
½ teaspoon salt
⅔ cup buttermilk
¼ cup maple syrup
¼ cup water
2 eggs
1 cup fresh blueberries

LET'S GET STARTED!

1. Preheat the oven to 375°F. Line 12 cups of a muffin tin with paper liners.
2. In a large bowl, whisk together the flour, sugar, baking powder, baking soda, and salt.
3. In a medium bowl, whisk together the buttermilk, maple syrup, water, and eggs.
4. Make a well in the center of the flour mixture and add the wet mixture. Stir just until no dry streaks of flour remain (do not overmix).
5. Fold in the blueberries.
6. Fill each paper liner two-thirds full with batter and bake until a wooden pick inserted into the center of a muffin comes out clean, 14 to 16 minutes.
7. Transfer to a wire rack to cool.

PB&J COOKIES

MAKES 3 DOZEN SANDWICH COOKIES

Peanut butter and jelly sandwiches were a staple in my house for school lunches. My mom would make me a different sandwich each day of the week and I loved the PB&J days. Now you can experience these same delicious flavors in cookie form! The slices of "bread" are peanut butter cookies, which pair wonderfully with your favorite jam. I prefer strawberry.

THE THINGS YOU'LL NEED

Peanut Butter Cookies
2 sticks (8 ounces) unsalted butter, at room temperature
1 cup creamy peanut butter
1 cup packed light brown sugar
1 cup granulated sugar
1 large egg
1 teaspoon baking soda
1 teaspoon baking powder
1 teaspoon vanilla extract
2½ cups all-purpose flour

Decorations
½ cup strawberry jam or jelly
Peanut butter (optional; see Ro Tip)

Equipment
1½-inch square cookie cutter
(template on page 251)

LET'S GET STARTED!

1. Preheat the oven to 350°F. Line 3 baking sheets with parchment paper.
2. In a medium bowl using a wooden spoon, mix the butter, peanut butter, brown sugar, and granulated sugar until smooth. Mix in the egg until well combined.
3. Add the baking soda, baking powder, and vanilla and mix well.
4. Stir in the flour until no dry streaks of flour remain.
5. On a lightly floured surface, roll out the dough to ¼ inch thick. Cut out cookies using the square cookie cutter.
6. Mold the squares into cookies shaped like slices of bread. Indent the center of the cookies to create a raised border all around.
7. Place the cookies 1 inch apart on the baking sheets.
8. Freeze for 10 minutes.
9. Bake until the cookies are firm to the touch but not browned at the edges, 6 to 8 minutes.
10. Let cool on the baking sheets for 2 minutes, then transfer to a wire rack to cool completely.

TIME TO DECORATE!

1. Scoop jam onto the smooth indented side of the cookies.

RO TIP

Sometimes I like to spread a little PEANUT BUTTER onto some of the cookies and make mini PB&J sandwiches!

FRUIT GUMMIES

MAKES 10 DOZEN GUMMIES

My elementary school teacher asked me what my favorite subject in school was and I answered "Snack time!" Whether it's before, during, or after school, it's always a good time to enjoy these fruity snacks. Their shape can be changed using any silicone mold you'd like; I used the one from my baking line.

THE THINGS YOU'LL NEED

Grape Gummies
1 cup grape juice
2 tablespoons unflavored gelatin
2 tablespoons maple syrup

Orange Gummies
1 cup orange juice
2 tablespoons unflavored gelatin
2 tablespoons maple syrup

Strawberry Gummies
1 cup pureed strawberries
2 tablespoons unflavored gelatin
2 tablespoons honey

Equipment
Silicone candy molds (Ro Baking Line by Wilton)
Squeeze bottle or dropper

LET'S GET STARTED!

Grape Gummies

1. Grease the silicone candy molds with cooking spray.
2. In a small saucepan, mix the grape juice, gelatin, and maple syrup. Mix well to remove any lumps. Allow the gelatin to bloom until thickened, about 5 minutes.
3. Place the saucepan over medium heat and bring to a simmer, whisking occasionally.
4. Remove from the heat and let cool slightly, about 5 minutes. Using a squeeze bottle or dropper, fill each mold cavity.
5. Refrigerate until the gummies are set, about 1 hour.
6. Pop the gummies out of the molds and store in an airtight container in the refrigerator for up to a week.

Orange Gummies

For the orange gummies, repeat steps 1 through 6 using the orange juice and maple syrup.

Strawberry Gummies

For the strawberry gummies, repeat steps 1 through 6 using the strawberry puree and honey.

GRADUATION CAP
CUPCAKES

MAKES 16 CUPCAKES

Congratulations! Graduation day is here and it's time to celebrate with cupcakes. These are decadent chocolate with a peanut butter filling. Blue and gold were my school colors, but these could be used for any elementary, middle, high school, and even college. Easily change the cupcake liners and sprinkles to show your school spirit.

THE THINGS YOU'LL NEED

Chocolate Cake
1½ cups all-purpose flour
¼ cup unsweetened cocoa powder
1 cup granulated sugar
1 teaspoon baking soda
½ teaspoon baking powder
½ teaspoon salt
½ cup half-and-half
¼ cup vegetable oil
1 large egg
½ teaspoon vanilla extract
½ cup water

Peanut Butter Filling
⅓ cup creamy peanut butter
⅓ cup powdered sugar
¼ cup half-and-half
¼ teaspoon vanilla extract

Decorations
1 batch Swiss Buttercream Frosting
    (page 17)
Blue sprinkles (or sprinkles in your
    school colors)
Miniature peanut butter cups
    (Reese's)
Milk chocolate squares (TCHO)
Small blue (or your school colors)
    candy-coated chocolates
    (M&M's Minis)

Equipment
Decorating tips: #1A, #1

LET'S GET STARTED!

1. Preheat the oven to 350°F. Line 16 cups of 2 muffin tins with foil liners.
2. Make the chocolate cake: In a large bowl, whisk together the flour, cocoa powder, granulated sugar, baking soda, baking powder, and salt.
3. In a medium bowl, whisk together the half-and-half, oil, egg, vanilla, and water.
4. Make a well in the center of the flour mixture and add the wet mixture. Stir just until no dry streaks of flour remain (do not overmix).
5. Fill the foil liners two-thirds full with batter.
6. Make the peanut butter filling: In a medium bowl, mix together the peanut butter and powdered sugar until smooth.
7. Add the half-and-half and vanilla and mix well.
8. Scoop the filling into a decorating bag and cut the tip. Pipe 1 tablespoon into the batter in each liner and swirl with a toothpick or skewer.
9. Bake until a wooden pick inserted into the center of a cupcake comes out clean, about 15 minutes.
10. Transfer to a wire rack to cool.

TIME TO DECORATE!

1. Make the Swiss Buttercream Frosting. Scoop it into a decorating bag fitted with a #1A tip and pipe a dome of frosting onto each cupcake. Reserve the remaining frosting for more decoration.
2. Roll the outer edge of the frosting in sprinkles.
3. Place a mini peanut butter cup upside down in the center of each cupcake. With a dab of frosting, attach the chocolate squares.
4. Scoop the remaining frosting into a decorating bag fitted with a #1 tip.
5. Using frosting, attach M&M's Minis on the center of the chocolate squares.
6. Pipe a tassel on the caps.

SAVE-THE-DATE
COOKIES

MAKES 2 DOZEN COOKIES

Send an edible Save the Date that your friends and family won't forget. Customize them with the special date on the front and decorate with your wedding colors.

THE THINGS YOU'LL NEED

Lemon Sablé Cookies
2 cups all-purpose flour
Grated zest of 1 lemon
¼ teaspoon sea salt
12 tablespoons (1½ sticks) unsalted
    butter, at room temperature
¾ cup powdered sugar, sifted
2 large egg yolks
2 teaspoons vanilla extract

Decorations
2 batches Royal Icing (page 16)
Food coloring: teal and black

Equipment
2½-inch square cookie cutter
    (template on page 251)
Decorating tips: #3, two #1

RO TIP

You can use your EVENT
COLORS to decorate!

LET'S GET STARTED!

1. In a medium bowl, whisk together the flour, lemon zest, and salt.
2. In a large bowl, with an electric mixer, beat the butter and powdered sugar until light and fluffy, 3 to 5 minutes.
3. Add the egg yolks one at a time, beating well after each addition. Scrape down the sides and bottom of the bowl as needed.
4. Beat in the vanilla.
5. On low speed, slowly beat in the flour mixture until combined.
6. Shape the dough into a disk and wrap in plastic wrap. Refrigerate for at least 1 hour.
7. Preheat the oven to 325°F. Line 2 baking sheets with parchment paper.
8. On a lightly floured surface, roll out the dough to ¼ inch thick. Cut out cookies using the square cookie cutter and place them 1 inch apart on the baking sheets.
9. Freeze for 10 minutes.
10. Bake until firm to the touch but not browned at the edges, 12 to 15 minutes.
11. Let cool on the baking sheets for 2 minutes, then transfer to a wire rack to cool completely.

TIME TO DECORATE!

1. Make the Royal Icing. Leave half the icing white and scoop into a decorating bag fitted with a #3 tip. Divide the other half into 2 bowls. Tint one bowl teal and the other gray. Scoop the icings into separate decorating bags fitted with #1 tips.
2. Outline the cookies with the white icing, then fill in the centers. Let the icing harden for about 1 hour.
3. Pipe a gray heart on each cookie. Pipe calendar grids around the hearts.
4. Use the teal icing to pipe the date: the month and year across the top, and the day in the heart.

WEDDING CAKE

Create lifelong memories with this clean, simple, and rustic wedding cake recipe that remains beautiful while maintaining a focus on flavor. The refreshing lemon cakes paired with the silky Swiss buttercream form a mouthwatering and crowd-pleasing experience.

THE THINGS YOU'LL NEED

Lemon Cake

6 cups all-purpose flour
2 tablespoons plus 2 teaspoons baking powder
2 teaspoons salt
4 sticks (16 ounces) unsalted butter, at room temperature
½ cup vegetable shortening
5 cups sugar
8 large eggs
2 teaspoons almond extract
2 teaspoons lemon extract
2 teaspoons grated lemon zest
2 cups half-and-half

Decorations

3 batches Swiss Buttercream Frosting (page 17)
Fresh flowers (optional)
Cake topper (optional)

Equipment

Two 4-inch round cake pans
Two 6-inch round cake pans
Two 8-inch round cake pans
Stand mixer fitted with the paddle attachment
Cake boards: 4-, 6-, and 8-inch
Large straws or cake dowels

LET'S GET STARTED!

1. Preheat the oven to 325°F. Grease two 4-inch, two 6-inch, and two 8-inch cake pans and line the bottoms with rounds of parchment paper.
2. In a medium bowl, whisk together the flour, baking powder, and salt.
3. In a stand mixer fitted with the paddle attachment, beat the butter, shortening, and sugar until light and fluffy, 3 to 5 minutes.
4. Add the eggs one at a time, beating well after each addition.
5. Beat in the almond extract, lemon extract, and lemon zest.
6. On low speed, alternate adding the flour mixture and the half-and-half to the butter mixture, beginning and ending with the flour mixture.
7. Divide the batter evenly among the prepared pans and bake until a wooden pick inserted into the center comes out clean: 25 to 30 minutes for the 4-inch cakes; about 50 minutes for the 6- and 8-inch cakes.
8. Let cool in the pans for 15 minutes, then turn out onto wire racks to cool completely.
9. Level off the tops with a cake leveler or a large serrated knife.
10. Cut each cake in half horizontally, creating four cake layers of each size.

• CONTINUES •

WEDDING

TIME TO DECORATE!

1. Make the Swiss Buttercream Frosting. Scoop it into a decorating bag and cut a large hole at the tip.
2. Stack the 4-inch cakes on the 4-inch cake board with frosting between the layers  (A). Repeat with the 6- and 8-inch cakes and cake boards.
3. Crumb coat each tier with a thin layer of frosting. Refrigerate for 30 minutes.
4. Pipe a thick layer of frosting onto the cakes and smooth with an offset spatula.
5. Lightly drag the tip of an offset spatula around the sides of the cake to create continuous horizontal lines (B).
6. Refrigerate the cakes for 30 minutes.
7. Cut 5 large straws to the height of the 6-inch tier and another 5 to the height of the 8-inch tier. Place the straws in the center of those tiers in a square pattern, with one in the center for support (C).
8. Place the 8-inch tier on a sturdy serving dish. Top with the 6-inch tier and finish with the 4-inch tier on top (D).
9. Optional: Decorate the cake with flowers and a cake topper.

▸ RO **TIP** ◂

Use a cake turntable
for SMOOTH,
continuous lines.

MONOGRAM
COOKIES

MAKES 2 DOZEN COOKIES

Personalized monogram cookies are perfect for engagement parties and bridal showers, or as wedding favors. Elegantly showcase two coming together with these almond-lavender shortbread confections.

THE THINGS YOU'LL NEED

Almond-Lavender Shortbread Cookies
1½ cups all-purpose flour
½ cup almond meal
¼ teaspoon sea salt
2 teaspoons finely chopped dried lavender
2 sticks (8 ounces) unsalted butter, at room temperature
½ cup sugar
1 teaspoon almond extract

Decorations
2 batches Royal Icing (page 16)
Food coloring: deep pink, red, and forest green
Edible white candy pearls
Almond extract (or any clear extract)
Edible gold dust

Equipment
Decorative plaque cookie cutters (templates on page 250)
2½-inch round cookie cutter (template on page 251)
Decorating tips: #3, two #1, #14, #16
Small paintbrush

LET'S GET STARTED!

1. In a medium bowl, whisk together the all-purpose flour, almond meal, salt, and lavender.
2. In a large bowl, with an electric mixer, beat the butter and sugar until light and fluffy, 3 to 5 minutes.
3. Beat in the almond extract.
4. On low speed, slowly beat in the flour mixture until combined.
5. Shape the dough into a disk and wrap in plastic wrap. Refrigerate for at least 1 hour.
6. Preheat the oven to 325°F. Line 2 baking sheets with parchment paper.
7. On a lightly floured surface, roll out the dough to ¼ inch thick. Cut out cookies using the decorative plaque and round cookie cutters and place them 2 inches apart on baking sheets.
8. Freeze for 10 minutes.
9. Bake until firm to the touch but not browned at the edges, 15 to 18 minutes.
10. Let cool on the baking sheets for 2 minutes, then transfer to a wire rack to cool completely.

TIME TO DECORATE!

1. Make the Royal Icing. Scoop half the icing into a decorating bag fitted with a #3 tip. Divide the remaining icing among 4 bowls:
   Bowl 1: Tint dark pink and scoop into a bag fitted with a #1 tip.
   Bowl 2: Tint light pink and scoop into a bag fitted with a #14 tip.
   Bowl 3: Tint red and scoop into a bag fitted with a #16 tip.
   Bowl 4: Tint green and scoop into a bag fitted with a #1 tip.
2. Outline the cookies with the white icing, then fill in the centers. Let the icing harden for about 1 hour.
3. Pipe white letters in the center of the cookies.
4. Pipe flowers with the dark pink, light pink, and red icing. Add pearls for decoration.
5. Pipe green icing around the flowers for leaf designs.
6. In a small bowl, mix the clear extract and edible gold dust. Once the letters have hardened, use the brush to paint them gold.

CHAMPAGNE
COOKIES

Toast the happy couple by raising your champagne glass cookies! They have all the flavor of sparkling wine without the alcohol, so kids and adults can enjoy them together.

THE THINGS YOU'LL NEED

Champagne Cookies

2¼ cups all-purpose flour

½ teaspoon baking powder

½ teaspoon salt

12 tablespoons (1½ sticks) unsalted butter, at room temperature

1 cup powdered sugar

1 large egg

2 tablespoons corn syrup

2½ teaspoons sparkling wine extract

Decorations

1 batch Royal Icing (page 16)

Fine gold sanding sugar

White pearl sprinkles

Equipment

4½-inch champagne flute cookie cutter (template on page 251)

#3 decorating tip

LET'S GET STARTED!

1. Make the champagne cookies: In a medium bowl, whisk together the flour, baking powder, and salt.
2. In a large bowl, with an electric mixer, beat the butter and powdered sugar until light and fluffy, 3 to 5 minutes.
3. Add the egg and corn syrup and beat well.
4. Beat in the sparkling wine extract.
5. On low speed, beat in the flour mixture until combined.
6. Shape the dough into a disk and wrap in plastic wrap. Refrigerate for at least 1 hour.
7. Preheat the oven to 350°F. Line 2 baking sheets with parchment paper.
8. On a lightly floured surface, roll out the dough to ¼ inch thick. Cut out cookies using the champagne flute cookie cutter and place them 1 inch apart on the baking sheets.
9. Bake until the cookies are firm to the touch but not browned at the edges, about 14 minutes.
10. Let cool on the baking sheets for 2 minutes, then transfer to a wire rack to cool completely.

TIME TO DECORATE!

1. Make the Royal Icing. Scoop it into a decorating bag fitted with a #3 tip.
2. Outline the cookies with the icing, then fill in the centers. Let the icing harden for about 1 hour.
3. Pipe a second layer of icing in the shape of the champagne. While the icing is still wet, cover with sanding sugar.
4. Using a dab of icing, place pearl sprinkles on the cookie to look like bubbles.

GENDER REVEAL
OMBRÉ CAKE

Gender reveal parties are taking place all around me. What happened? When did I become an adult? It's exciting to learn the gender of a loved one's baby, and cakes are one of the most popular ways to do so. This cake is decorated with a pink and blue ombré on the outside and baby's gender color on the inside.

THE THINGS YOU'LL NEED

Vanilla Cake
1 cup all-purpose flour
1 cup cake flour
1 teaspoon baking powder
¾ teaspoon baking soda
½ teaspoon salt
8 tablespoons (1 stick) unsalted butter
1 cup granulated sugar
2 large eggs
½ teaspoon vanilla extract
½ teaspoon almond extract
1 cup buttermilk
Pink or blue food coloring

Decorations
1 batch Swiss Buttercream Frosting (page 17)
Pink and blue food coloring
Pink and blue pearl sprinkles
Sanding sugar: pink and blue

LET'S GET STARTED!

1. Preheat the oven to 325°F. Grease three 6-inch round cake pans and line the bottoms with rounds of parchment paper.
2. In a medium bowl, whisk together the all-purpose flour, cake flour, baking powder, baking soda, and salt.
3. In a large bowl, with an electric mixer, beat the butter and granulated sugar until light and fluffy, 3 to 5 minutes.
4. Add the eggs one at a time, beating well after each addition.
5. Beat in the vanilla and almond extract.
6. On low speed, alternate adding the flour mixture and the buttermilk to the butter mixture, beginning and ending with the flour mixture.
7. Tint the batter pink or blue for the gender reveal.
8. Divide the batter evenly among the prepared pans and bake until a wooden pick inserted into the center comes out clean, 30 to 35 minutes.
9. Let cool in the pans for 15 minutes, then turn out onto a wire rack to cool completely.
10. Level off the tops with a cake leveler or a large serrated knife to create three 1-inch-tall layers.

• CONTINUES •

BABY SHOWER

1. Make the Swiss Buttercream Frosting. Divide it among 3 bowls. Tint one bowl pink, one blue, and leave one untinted. Scoop the pink and blue frostings into separate decorating bags and cut the tips.
2. Stack the cakes with a thin layer of untinted buttercream frosting in between the layers.
3. Crumb coat the cake with a thin layer of untinted frosting. Refrigerate the cake for 30 minutes.
4. Pipe pink frosting around the bottom half of the cake and blue frosting around the top half and over the top of the cake **A**.
5. Using an offset spatula, smooth the frosting in one direction around the cake to create an ombré effect **B**.
6. Using the offset spatula, pull the overhanging edges toward the center of the cake and smooth **C**.
7. Top with sprinkles and sanding sugar **D**.

> RO **TIP**

Use a cake
TURNTABLE to help
smooth the
frosting evenly.

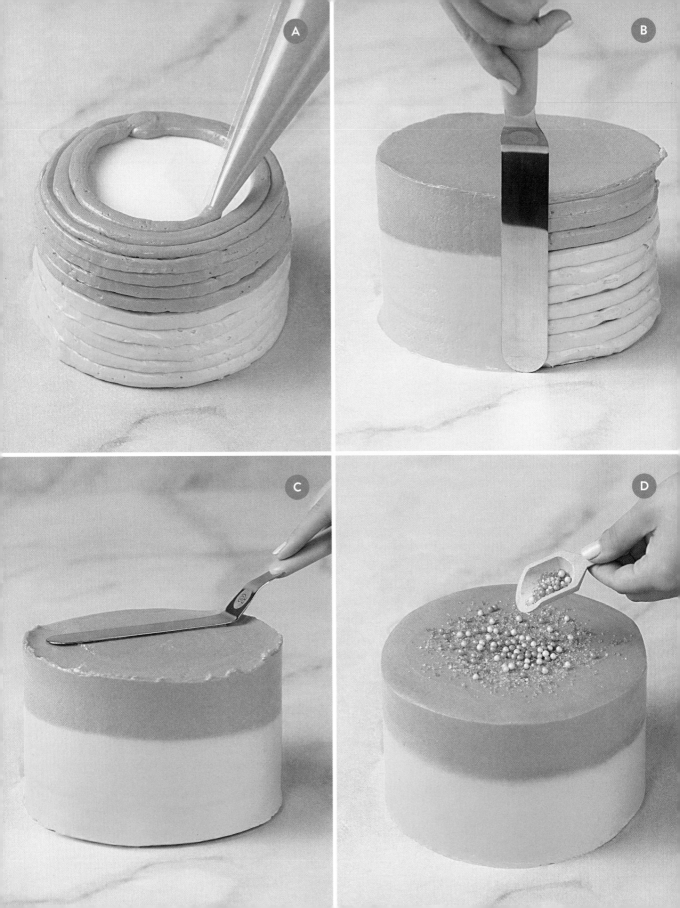

PIÑATA COOKIES

MAKES 14 COOKIES

What will baby be? There are many exciting ways to tell your family and friends the gender of your baby, and these piñata cookies are a super fun option. They can even be shipped to those who can't make it to the gender reveal party.

THE THINGS YOU'LL NEED

Cream Cheese Sugar Cookies
3 cups all-purpose flour
1 teaspoon baking powder
½ teaspoon salt
2 sticks (8 ounces) unsalted butter, at room temperature
2 ounces cream cheese, at room temperature
1 cup sugar
1 large egg
1 large egg yolk
1½ teaspoons vanilla extract

Decorations
1 batch Royal Icing (page 16)
Food coloring: yellow, orange, and black
Pink or blue pearl sprinkles

Equipment
Duck cookie cutter (template on page 251)
Decorating tips: #3, three #2

LET'S GET STARTED!

1. Make the cream cheese sugar cookies: In a medium bowl, whisk together the flour, baking powder, and salt.
2. In a large bowl, with an electric mixer, beat the butter, cream cheese, and sugar until light and fluffy, 3 to 5 minutes.
3. Add the whole egg and egg yolk one at a time, beating well after each addition.
4. Beat in the vanilla.
5. On low speed, beat in the flour mixture until combined.
6. Shape the dough into a disk and wrap in plastic wrap. Refrigerate for at least 1 hour.
7. Preheat the oven to 350°F. Line 4 baking sheets with parchment paper.
8. On a lightly floured surface, roll out the dough to ¼ inch thick. Cut out 42 cookies using the duck cookie cutter. Cut out the centers from one-third of the cookies Ⓐ. Place the cookies 1 inch apart on the baking sheets.
9. Freeze the cookies for 15 minutes.
10. Bake until the cookies are firm to the touch but not browned at the edges, 10 to 12 minutes.
11. Let cool on the baking sheets for 2 minutes, then transfer to a wire rack to cool completely.

• CONTINUES •

1. Make the Royal Icing. Scoop three-quarters of the icing into a bowl, tint yellow, then scoop into a decorating bag fitted with a #3 tip.
2. Divide the remaining icing among 3 bowls. Tint one bowl black, one orange, and leave one untinted. Scoop the icings into separate decorating bags fitted with #2 tips.
3. Using the yellow icing, outline half the full (uncut) cookies, skipping the beak. Fill in the centers and let dry completely. Pipe wing details **B**.
4. Pipe beaks with the orange icing.
5. Pipe eyes with the white icing. Once dry, pipe pupils with the black icing **C**.
6. Pipe icing around the edge of a full undecorated cookie and stack a cutout cookie on top. Fill with sprinkles. Pipe icing around the edge and stack a decorated cookie on top **D**. Press to seal.

READY TO POP!
CARAMEL CORN

───── **MAKES 7 TO 8 CUPS** ─────

These sweet and salty treats are perfect for any craving and also to give out as party favors. A wonderful recipe to make for a baby shower.

THE THINGS YOU'LL NEED

Caramel Corn

1 tablespoon oil
¼ cup popcorn kernels
4 tablespoons unsalted butter
½ cup sugar
2 teaspoons lemon juice
½ teaspoon vanilla extract
¼ teaspoon salt
Pinch of baking soda

Equipment

Large pot with a lid
Small heavy-bottomed pan (do not use a nonstick pan)
Candy thermometer
Treat bags
Pink and blue ribbons
"Ready to Pop!" stickers (template on RosannaPansino.com)

LET'S GET STARTED!

1. Preheat the oven to 300°F. Line a baking sheet with parchment paper and grease the paper.
2. Heat a large pot over medium heat for 1 to 3 minutes. Add the oil and heat for 10 seconds, then add 3 popcorn kernels.
3. Once the kernels pop, add the remaining kernels. Cover with a lid and gently shake the pot to coat the kernels with the oil. When popping begins, gently shake the pot continuously over the heat until the popping begins to slow, about 1 minute.
4. Remove from the heat and transfer the popcorn to a large heatproof bowl.
5. In a small heavy-bottomed pan fitted with a candy thermometer, combine the butter, sugar, and lemon juice and cook over medium heat to 275°F.
6. Remove from the heat and carefully stir in the vanilla, salt, and baking soda.
7. Pour the caramel mixture over the popcorn and mix until evenly coated.
8. Spread the caramel corn onto the prepared baking sheet and bake until the caramel begins to darken, 15 to 20 minutes.
9. Remove from the oven and immediately stir the caramel corn on the baking sheet. Let cool.

TIME TO DECORATE!

1. Package the caramel corn in treat bags.
2. Tie the bags with ribbon and stick on "Ready to Pop!" signs.

BABEE SHOWER CAKE

MAKES ONE 6-INCH THREE-LAYER CAKE

Whether for a baby shower or baby's first birthday, this buzzworthy cake is the bee's knees. On the inside is a delightful honey cake, which is simply decorated with honey buttercream frosting to look like a beehive. A wonderful confection for a mommy to bee!

THE THINGS YOU'LL NEED

Fondant
Fondant: yellow, black, and white

Honey Cake
2½ cups plus 2 tablespoons all-purpose flour
2¼ teaspoons baking powder
¼ teaspoon salt
12 tablespoons (1½ sticks) unsalted butter, at room temperature
1 cup plus 2 tablespoons sugar
¾ cup honey
3 large eggs
4½ teaspoons vanilla extract
¾ cup whole milk

Decorations
2 batches Honey Buttercream Frosting (page 19)
Food coloring: yellow and black
Black FoodWriter pen (Wilton)

Equipment
Small (1¹⁄₁₆-inch) teardrop cookie cutter (template on page 251)
Decorating tips: #809, two #12

FONDANT PREP!

1. Work with fondant on wax paper sprinkled with powdered sugar.
2. For the bee bodies, roll the yellow fondant into 1-inch oval balls. Roll out the black fondant to ⅛ inch thick and cut out strips ⅛ inch wide and 3 inches long. Attach to the bee bodies using water.
3. For the wings, roll out the white fondant to ⅛ inch thick and cut out small teardrops with the teardrop cookie cutter. Once hardened attach 2 wings to each bee body.
4. Draw eyes and eyelashes on each bee with a black FoodWriter pen Ⓐ.
5. Set aside to harden.

LET'S GET STARTED!

1. Preheat the oven to 350°F. Line the bottoms of three 6-inch round cake pans with rounds of parchment paper and heavily grease the paper.
2. Make the honey cake: In a medium bowl, whisk together the flour, baking powder, and salt.
3. In a large bowl, with an electric mixer, beat the butter, sugar, and honey until light and fluffy, 3 to 5 minutes
4. Add the eggs one at a time, beating well after each addition.
5. Beat in the vanilla.
6. On low speed, alternate adding the flour mixture and the milk to the butter mixture, beginning and ending with the flour mixture.
7. Divide the batter evenly among the prepared pans and bake until a wooden pick inserted into the center comes out clean, 45 to 50 minutes.
8. Let cool in the pans for 15 minutes, then turn out onto a wire rack to cool completely.

• CONTINUES •

9. Level off the tops of 2 cakes with a cake leveler or a large serrated knife; leave the third cake unleveled.

TIME TO DECORATE!

1. Make the Honey Buttercream Frosting. Scoop ¼ cup of the frosting into a small bowl and tint black, then scoop into a decorating bag fitted with a #12 tip. Tint the remaining frosting yellow and scoop a small amount into a decorating bag fitted with a #12 tip for step 8. Scoop the remaining yellow frosting into a decorating bag fitted with a #809 tip (you may have to refill it, depending on the size of your decorating bag).
2. Stack the cakes with thin layers of yellow buttercream frosting in between the layers and the unleveled cake on top.
3. Freeze the cake for 15 minutes to harden.
4. Using a serrated knife, carve the cake into a beehive shape **B**.
5. Crumb coat the cake with a thin layer of frosting. Refrigerate for 30 minutes.
6. Pipe a door with the black frosting **C**.
7. Pipe horizontal stripes of yellow frosting around the cake, starting from the bottom and working to the top, making a beehive texture **D**.
8. Using the decorating bag fitted with a #12 tip, pipe a border around the doorway.
9. Place the bees on the cake.

ACKNOWLEDGMENTS

CREATING MY SECOND COOKBOOK was as much
a labor of love for me as it was for many others. I cannot give them
enough thanks for their support in helping make this book.

First, I'd like to give thanks to my viewers, the Fansino Family, for showing me unwavering support and love. This project would not have been possible without you. You mean the world to me.

My culinary team, Robynne, Beryl, Kim, and Caitlin, for testing all of my recipe ideas and providing invaluable insight. Their talent is an inspiration to me.

Michael, the man behind the camera who always makes sure every recipe shot looks perfect, and Megan, who worked on the computer to ensure each final photo was exactly what I had envisioned.

My sister, Molly, who moved to California to help me with every aspect of my business and who keeps me organized, and my assistant, Stephanie, for jumping right into this project with nothing but pure excitement.

My stylist Kimmy, who found so many wonderful outfits on short notice, and Franco, who made sure everything fit my petite frame perfectly.

Diana, for always making me look my best, whether it's in this book, on TV, for my videos, or on a red carpet.

My editor at Atria Books, Johanna Castillo, for completely supporting me once again on my second book and for being open to every silly idea I have.

Erin, my literary agent, for helping put this book together, and my entire team at WME for supporting me in more ways than I can list.

Ryan, who still has my back and is one of my favorite people in the world.

Mike, my business partner, manager, and the most dedicated person I've ever known. Thank you for not running away when I said I wanted to do another book.

And lastly, I can't forget my dog, Cookie, not only for being a model in multiple photos, but also for putting a smile on my face every single day.

CONVERSION CHART

Measurements & Temperatures

CUP TO TABLESPOON TO TEASPOON TO MILLILITERS

1 cup = 16 tablespoons = 48 teaspoons = 240 ml

¾ cup = 12 tablespoons = 36 teaspoons = 180 ml

⅔ cup = 11 tablespoons = 32 teaspoons = 160 ml

½ cup = 8 tablespoons = 24 teaspoons = 120 ml

⅓ cup = 5 tablespoons = 16 teaspoons = 80 ml

¼ cup = 4 tablespoons = 12 teaspoons = 60 ml

1 tablespoon = 15 ml

1 teaspoon = 5 ml

CUP TO FLUID OUNCES

1 cup = 8 fluid ounces

¾ cup = 6 fluid ounces

⅔ cup = 5 fluid ounces

½ cup = 4 fluid ounces

⅓ cup = 3 fluid ounces

¼ cup = 2 fluid ounces

FAHRENHEIT TO CELSIUS (°F TO °C)

500°F = 260°C

475°F = 245°C

450°F = 235°C

425°F = 220°C

400°F = 205°C

375°F = 190°C

350°F = 180°C

325°F = 160°C

300°F = 150°C

275°F = 135°C

250°F = 120°C

225°F = 107°C

Basic Ingredients

ALL-PURPOSE FLOUR (UNSIFTED)

1 cup flour = 120 grams

¾ cup flour = 90 grams

½ cup flour = 60 grams

¼ cup flour = 30 grams

GRANULATED SUGAR

1 cup sugar = 200 grams

¾ cup sugar = 150 grams

⅔ cup sugar = 135 grams

½ cup sugar = 100 grams

⅓ cup sugar = 70 grams

¼ cup sugar = 50 grams

POWDERED SUGAR (UNSIFTED)

1 cup powdered sugar = 120 grams

¾ cup powdered sugar = 90 grams

½ cup powdered sugar = 60 grams

¼ cup powdered sugar = 30 grams

BUTTER

1 cup butter = 2 sticks = 8 ounces = 227 grams

½ cup butter = 1 stick = 4 ounces = 113 grams

HEAVY CREAM

1 cup heavy cream = 235 grams

¾ cup heavy cream = 175 grams

½ cup heavy cream = 115 grams

¼ cup heavy cream = 60 grams

1 tablespoon heavy cream = 15 grams

RESOURCE GUIDE

Bakeware Items Used in this Book

CUPCAKE CONE BAKING RACK
Wilton

PRINCESS CAKE PAN
Rosanna Pansino by Wilton

NERDY NUMMIES SILICONE CANDY MOLD
Rosanna Pansino by Wilton

GUMMY BEAR SILICONE MOLD
Rosanna Pansino by Wilton

6-INCH ROUND CAKE PAN
Rosanna Pansino by Wilton

MINI CUPCAKE PAN
Wilton

MINI FLUTED PAN
Wilton

WITCH FINGER PAN
Wilton

PASTA ROLLER
Marcato

PIZZA STONE
Cuisinart

8-INCH RING MOLD PAN
Fat Daddio's

Baking, Craft & Party Supply Stores

AMAZON.COM
www.amazon.com

CRATE & BARREL
www.crateandbarrel.com

JO-ANN FABRIC AND CRAFT STORES
www.joann.com

LAKELAND (UK)
www.lakeland.co.uk

MICHAELS THE ARTS AND CRAFTS STORE
www.michaels.com

PARTY CITY
www.partycity.com

SUR LA TABLE
www.surlatable.com

TARGET
www.target.com

WALMART
www.walmart.com

WILTON INDUSTRIES
www.wilton.com

TEMPLATES

HOLLY LEAF

REINDEER EYE

CONVERSATION HEART PETITS FOURS

HEART WHOOPIE PIES

HEART RAVIOLI

DAISY LEMON TARTS

STAR SCONES

SNOWY STAR BEIGNETS

BUNNY FEET

MUSTACHE DONUTS

JACK-O'-LANTERN COOKIE POPS

CORNCOB (HARVEST COOKIES)

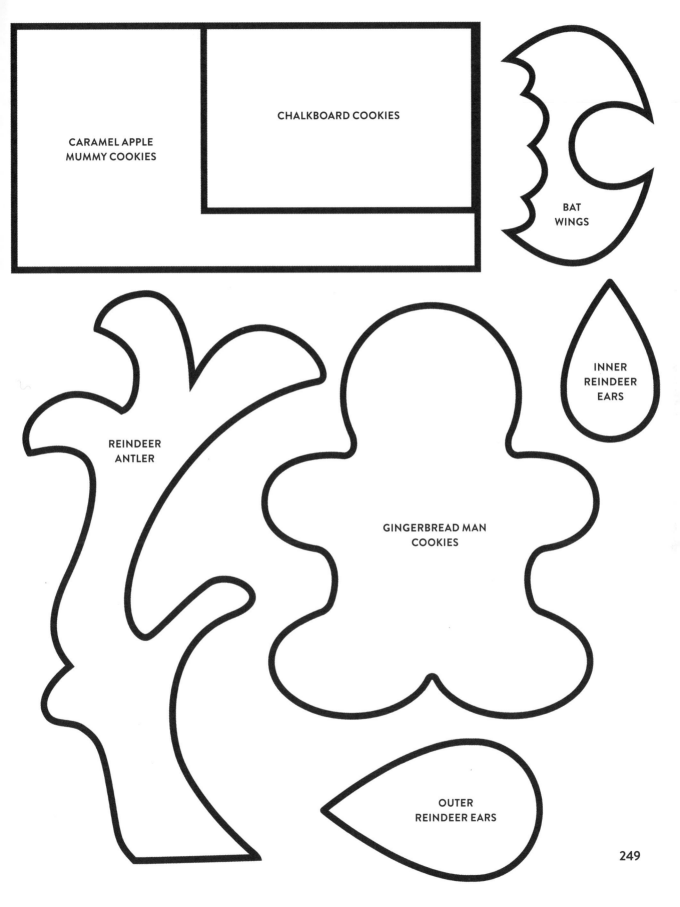

CARAMEL APPLE
MUMMY COOKIES

CHALKBOARD COOKIES

BAT
WINGS

INNER
REINDEER
EARS

REINDEER
ANTLER

GINGERBREAD MAN
COOKIES

OUTER
REINDEER EARS

249

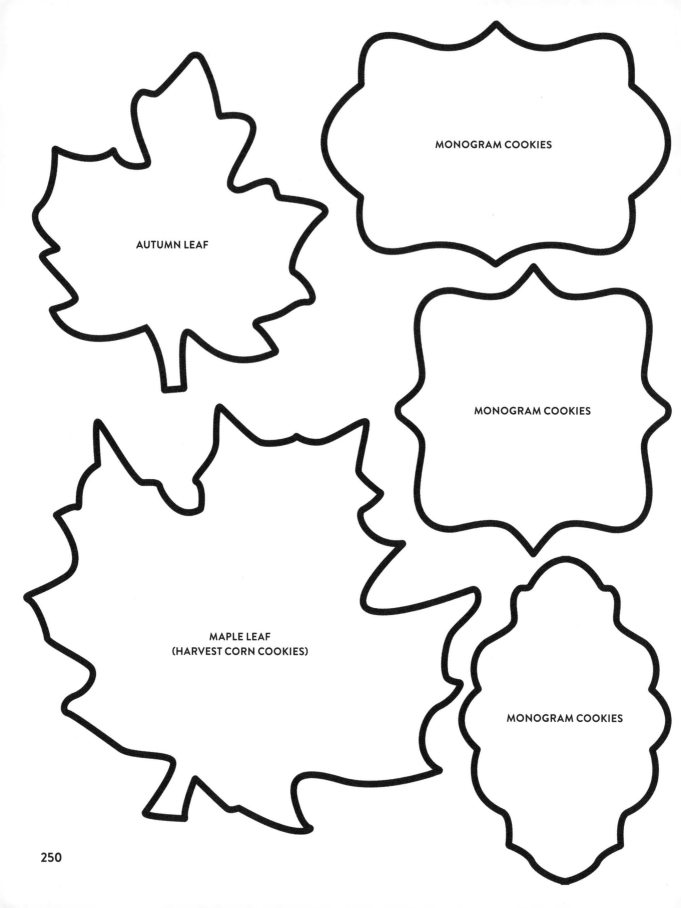

AUTUMN LEAF

MONOGRAM COOKIES

MONOGRAM COOKIES

MAPLE LEAF
(HARVEST CORN COOKIES)

MONOGRAM COOKIES

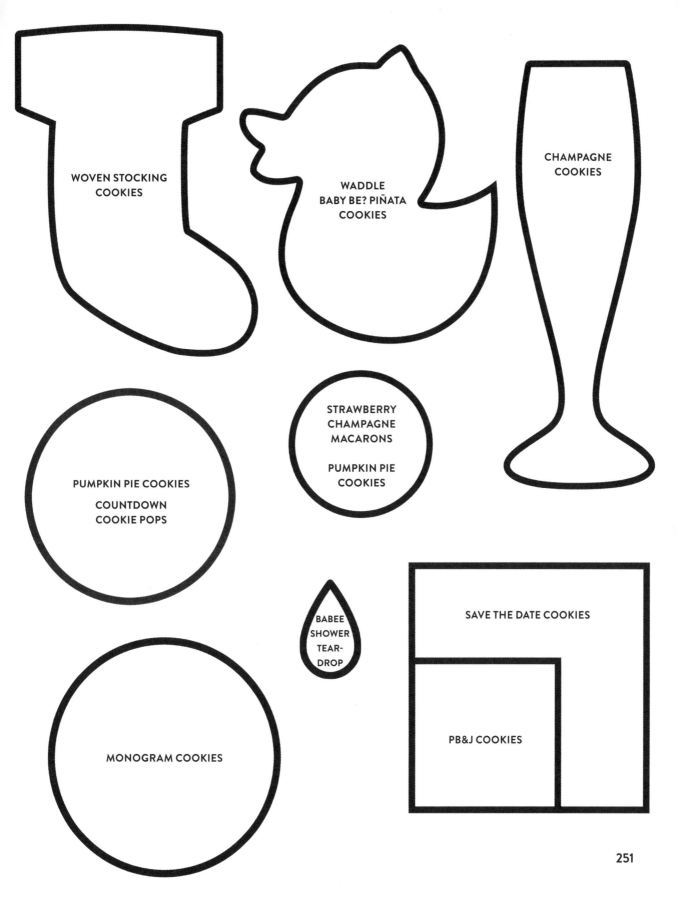

WOVEN STOCKING
COOKIES

WADDLE
BABY BE? PIÑATA
COOKIES

CHAMPAGNE
COOKIES

PUMPKIN PIE COOKIES

COUNTDOWN
COOKIE POPS

STRAWBERRY
CHAMPAGNE
MACARONS

PUMPKIN PIE
COOKIES

BABEE
SHOWER
TEAR-
DROP

SAVE THE DATE COOKIES

PB&J COOKIES

MONOGRAM COOKIES

INDEX

ABOUT THE AUTHOR

ROSANNA PANSINO
is an award-winning YouTube star, baker, entrepreneur, and author. Her first book, *The Nerdy Nummies Cookbook*, is a *New York Times* bestseller. She also created and hosts *Nerdy Nummies,* the internet's most popular baking show.

Pansino launched her YouTube channel in 2011 and since then her videos have been viewed more than 2.5 billion times. With more than 10 million subscribers, Rosanna is one of the most-watched and followed personalities on the internet.

In 2015, she executive produced and hosted two holiday food specials on the Cooking Channel. In 2017, she partnered with Wilton to launch her own branded line of baking tools and was named the Top Food Influencer of the year by *Forbes.*

She currently lives in Los Angeles with her family and dog, Cookie.

youtube.com/rosannapansino   @rosannapansino   facebook.com/rosannapansino   @rosannapansino   @rosannapansino